5s Home

By Ade Asefeso MCIPS MBA

Copyright 2013 by Ade Asefeso MCIPS MBA
All rights reserved.

ISBN 978-1-291-34524-7

Publisher: AA Global Sourcing Ltd
Website: http://www.aaglobalsourcing.com

Table of Contents

Disclaimer 5
Dedication 6
Chapter 1: Introduction...7
Chapter 2: Keep Lean Gurus Value to Perspective 11
Chapter 3: The Origins of 5s..15
Chapter 4: The Objectives of 5s...19
Chapter 5: Bringing 5s Home...23
Chapter 6: Visual Home/Office and 5s.....................................27
Chapter 7: 5S Housekeeping at Home 45
Chapter 8: Ways to Kill Clutter in 5 Minutes.............................51
Chapter 9: 5s Bedroom...55
Chapter 10: Kitchens Are Already Lean...................................57
Chapter 11: Attacking the Kitchen With 5s...............................59
Chapter 12: Kaizen Versus Kaizen Blitzes...............................69
Chapter 13: Poka Yoke and Childproofing................................73
Chapter 14: The 2 Types of Muda 77
Chapter 15: Seven Kinds of Waste 81
Chapter 16: Defects 85
Chapter 17: Inventory...89
Chapter 18: Motion...91
Chapter 19: Overprocessing 97
Chapter 20: Overproduction...101
Chapter 21: Transportation 105
Chapter 22: Waiting 111
Chapter 23: Kanban and Fine Tuning 115
Chapter 24: Little Guy Versus the Big Boss...........................119
Chapter 25: Toward a Lean Laundry 123
Chapter 26: Lean-ifying Laundry at Home 127

Chapter 27: Holiday Hangovers Aren't Productive.......................131
Chapter 28: Checking Up On Baby Bottles................................135
Chapter 29: Resources Are the Enemy 139
Chapter 30: Non-Lean Doctor's Office 141
Chapter 31: Conclusion..143
Resource and References 145

Disclaimer

This publication is designed to provide competent and reliable information regarding the subject matter covered. However, it is sold with the understanding that the author and publisher are not engaged in rendering professional advice. The authors and publishers specifically disclaim any liability that is incurred from the use or application of contents of this book.

If you purchased this book without a cover you should be aware that this book may have been stolen property and reported as "unsold and destroyed" to the publisher. In this case neither the author nor the publisher has received any payment for this "stripped book."

Dedication

This book is dedicated to the hundreds of thousands of incredible souls in the world who have weathered through the up and down of recent recession.

To my good friend and mentor Andy Hobbs who seems to have been sent here to teach me something about who I am supposed to be. He has nurtured me and my son Karl, challenged me, and even opposed me…. But at every juncture has taught me!

This book is dedicated to my lovely boys, Thomas, Michael and Karl. Teaching them to manage their finance will give them the lives they deserve. They have taught me more about life, presence, and energy management than anything I have done in my life.

Chapter 1: Introduction

I am writing this book because a lady that regularly buys and read my series of lean books with her husband wrote to me and said "My husband had a dream after reading your books and applying the principle to his business. He wants to 5S our home. We know how to 5S our business. How do we 5S our home?"

5S is a philosophy and a way of organizing and managing the workspace by eliminating waste; however we all have these wastes in our home and our day-to-day life.

The 5S is a list of five Japanese words that begin with 'S': Seiri, Seiton, Seiso, Seiketsu, Shitsuke. The closest English equivalent is Sort, Set, Shine, Standardize and Sustain.

5S is customarily implemented in connection with a Kaizen, lean manufacturing, or continuous improvement program. However, 5S can be a stand-alone program. Often, 5S is discussed in the context of Kaizen, Lean Production or Continuous Improvement techniques as used in manufacturing. Nevertheless, 5S should work in any environment; the workplace, your home, your PC filing system or even your own head.

The Benefits of 5S
- Greater efficiency in achieving goals
- Greater readiness for new tasks
- Fewer hazards
- Less spending on replacing lost or damaged items
- Less stress

- Greater self-esteem
- More space

The Practice of Sort
- Sort through everything in the workplace / home.
- Keep the essential.
- Store the useful.
- Discard everything else.
- Discarding should be without regret, for everything that is left should promote productivity.

The Benefits of Sort
- Fewer hazards
- Less clutter to interfere with productive work
- Simplification of tasks
- Effective use of space
- Careful purchasing of items

The Practice of Set in Order
- A place for everything and everything in its place.
- Organise and design in your home / workplace to promote efficiency.
- Arrange tools and materials in assigned places where they can be accessed quickly, thus promoting work flow.
- Keep tools and equipment where they will be used.
- Order items to eliminate 'extra motion'.
- Allocate a location to each item.
- Label each location to identify what is kept there.

The Benefits of Set in Order
- Good workflow equal achievement.

- When things can be found we have less frustration.

The Practice of Shine
- Keep your home / workplace clean as well as neat.
- See your environment workplace through the eyes of a visitor; keeping a high standard of cleanliness to make a good impression.
- Maintain cleanliness daily, not just occasionally.
- Make cleanliness a part of the work, not an extra.
- Cleaning is done by everyone.
- No area should be missed.

The Benefits of Shine
- A good impression
- Better health
- A better quality of life
- Improved self-esteem

The Practice of Standardize
- Operate consistently.
- Everyone must know their responsibilities.
- Use your five senses. Examples of using senses sometimes called "Visual Management"
- Make it easy to spot anomalies.
- Detect abnormalities and correct them immediately.
- Colour-coding.
- Outlining tools on a tool board.

The Practice of Sustain
- Finally, maintain standards. Learn not to need reminding about the 5S way.

- Make 5S's a way of life.
- Focus on the 5S way.
- Eliminate bad habits.

The Benefits of Sustain
- No gradual decline back to the previous way of operating.

Chapter 2: Keep Lean Gurus Value to Perspective

In this book, I think it's worth pointing out that I am not a "lean production guru." I am not a Six Sigma Blackbelt, I have not won the Deming or Shingo prizes, I am not Taiichi Ohno's favourite caddy, or anything like that.

I am just a guy who's excited about lean organization principles, and I'm trying to figure out how to make them work in people's personal lives as well as they work in a car factory.

Is it a problem that I'm not a big-time lean production guru? That depends. When it comes to expertise, you hear two different things about lean production.

It takes years of experience, either at a classic lean organization like Toyota or in the apprenticeship of a lean master (or both), to truly master totally different way of thinking that lean production is all about.

Lean production is a process, not a product. Everyone has something to contribute to this process, no matter how little or how much experience they may have with it.

A Lean guru who I will not mention his name once said. "It takes ten years to truly master the Toyota Production System (TPS). At another point, the same guru quotes his TPS mentor saying that "Toyota's production system is not "THE TOYOTA PRODUCTION SYSTEM." (That is, the TPS and the lean principles it describes are an ideal to be sought after, not an accurate depiction of how the Toyota company runs in real life. Even Toyota has not truly mastered the Toyota System.)

What are we to make of this? Is it worth the effort to grapple with lean production ideas if you aren't a master of them? What place should these ideas have in our everyday lives?

Perhaps a good metaphor for TPS and lean production is human DNA: We all have DNA in every cell in our bodies, and these copies of DNA are essentially instruction books for how to make a human being. All you have to do is follow the instructions, and, boom, there's a person.

But in real life, it's obviously more complicated than that. Gestating, being born, growing, and maturing are extremely complicated processes, processes that are extremely sensitive to the raw materials they are fed and the external conditions under which they take place. Furthermore, following the instructions encoded in DNA is just the beginning: Figuring out how to continuously grow and adapt to an environment full of rapidly changing resources, hazards, and information is much trickier. DNA only tells you a small part of the story about the person you see in front of you.

Likewise, the lean production principles described in the TPS (and elsewhere) are just the DNA for lean organizations. They are very useful guidelines and contain some profound truths, but they are still just the beginning. Figuring out how to put these ideas to work in your everyday circumstances to continuously achieve higher-quality, more-satisfying, less-wasteful outcomes is a challenge that will always be somewhat different for each person trying to do it.

There is a famous book on psychotherapy called "If You Meet The Buddha In The Road, Kill Him." Its point (so I've heard) is that the real work of psychological growth has to be done by the individual, not by their therapist. Forgetting that, and depending on gurus to do the work that only you can do to make your life better, leads to trouble. (No, you aren't supposed to actually kill the gurus, just keep their value to you in perspective.)

So yes, pay attention to what the lean gurus out there have to say if it's useful to you (including, if you want, my own struggles with these ideas). But remember that the real work of creating leaner processes in your everyday life is yours and yours alone.

Chapter 3: The Origins of 5s

5S was developed in Japan. It was first heard of as one of the techniques that enabled what was then termed 'Just in Time Manufacturing'. The Massachusetts Institute of Technology's 5-year study into the future of the automobile in the late 1980s identified that the term was inappropriate since the Japanese success was built upon far more than components arriving only at the time of requirement. John Krafcik, a researcher on the project, ascribed Lean to the collective techniques being used in Japanese automobile manufacturing; it reflected the focus on waste in all its forms that was central to the Japanese approach. Minimised inventory was only one aspect of performance levels in companies such as Toyota and in itself only arose from progress in fields such as quality assurance to highlight problems for immediate action.

5S was developed by Hiroyuki Hirano within his overall approach to production systems. Many Western managers coming across the approach for the first time found the experience one of enlightenment. They had perhaps always known the role of housekeeping within optimised manufacturing performance and had always known the elements of best practice. However, Hirano provided a structure for improvement programs. He pointed out a series of identifiable steps, each building on its predecessor. Western managers, for example, had always recognised the need to decide upon locations for materials and tools and upon the flow of work through a work area; central to this (but perhaps implicit) is the principle that items not essential to the process should be removed stored elsewhere or eliminated completely. By differentiating between Sort and Set, Hirano made the distinction explicit. He taught his audience that any effort to consider layout and flow before the removal of the unnecessary items was likely to lead to a sub-optimal solution.

Equally the Shine, or cleanliness, phase is a distinct element of the change program that can transform a process area. Hirano's view is that the definition of a cleaning methodology (Set) is a discrete activity, not to be confused with the organisation of the workplace, and this helps to structure any improvement program. It has to be recognised, however, that there is inevitably an overlap between Set and Shine. Western managers understood that the opportunities for various cleanliness methodologies vary with the layout and storage mechanisms adopted. However, breaking down the improvement activity in this way clarifies that the requirements for the cleanliness regime must be understood as a factor in the design aspect of Set. Toyota's adoption of the Hirano approach is '4S', with Set and Shine combined presumably for this very reason. The improvement team must avoid the trap of designing the work area and then considering the cleanliness or tidiness mechanism.

Hirano also reminded the world of the Hawthorne effect. We can all introduce change and while people in the business consider the change program to be under management focus the benefits of the change will continue, but when this focus has moved (as is inevitably the case) performance once more slips. Western managers, in particular, may have benefited from the distinction between the procedural or mechanical elements, Standardisation, of keeping these matters in focus and the culture change, Sustain, which is a distinct approach to bringing about a new way of working. A number of publications on the subject in the West have questioned whether this culture can really be tackled as part of an exercise of relatively limited scope. The broader kaizen, or continuous improvement, approach is built, among other things, upon the company's valuation of all members of the workforce. If employees don't feel valued within the overall company culture, perhaps the change required falls outside the limits of a housekeeping improvement program.

Chapter 4: The Objectives of 5s

Hirano identified a range of benefits from improved housekeeping, all of which can be regarded as falling within the Lean portfolio – that is, they are all based around the elimination of waste in one form or another.

The most obvious benefit from items being organized in such a way (i.e. that they are always readily available) is that of improved productivity. Production workers being diverted from production to look for tools, gauges, production paperwork, fasteners, and so on is the most frustrating form of lost time in any plant. A key aspect of Hirano's organisation approach is that the often-needed items are stored in the most accessible location and correct adoption of the standardisation approach means that they are returned to the correct location after use.

Another element of Hirano's improved housekeeping is improved plant maintenance; workers 'owning' a piece of plant, responsible for keeping it clean and tidy, can take ownership for highlighting potential problems before they have an impact on performance. (Of course, this brings with it the interface with preventive maintenance and the need for clarity in the 'assignment map', that is; who does what. The division of tasks between production workers and specialist maintenance engineers varies with the nature of the business, but ownership rests within the business unit rather than within the 'service provider'.)

The next aim is Quality. The degree of impact of dirt in a manufacturing environment, obviously, varies with the nature of the product and its process but there are few, if any, areas where dirt is welcome. Even if it is only in the form of soiled documentation accompanying the goods to the customer this can send a very negative message about the company and its culture.

In other cases dirt can have a serious impact on product performance either directly or indirectly, perhaps through compromising the integrity of test processes. Of course, 5S does more than address dirt; an inappropriate layout can result, for example, in product damaged through excessive movement or through the use of tooling other than that defined as the standard. Standardisation is a theme of Hirano's approach, overlapping to a considerable extent with, for example, that of Ohno. A Standard Operating Procedure for tool certification is much easier to achieve if the tool to be certified is always in a clearly-marked location.

Another goal is improved Health and Safety. Clear pathways between workbenches and storage racks can minimise accidents, as can properly-swept floors. As with Quality, a well-organised, clean and tidy facility lends itself more readily to standard practice. Hirano also described how an environment in which the workforce has pride in their workplace can contribute to a considerable extent in a number of ways including customer service. Improving the layout of the facility merges with the concept of visual management; if workers can see the status of plant and of work in the facility, thus removing the need for complex tracking and communication systems, then benefits will accrue. 5S can also be a valuable sales tool when potential customers visit; a well-organised, clean and tidy facility sends a message of a professional and well-organised supplier.

One point made by all practitioners is that the adoption of 5S must be driven by goals. The successful implementation of 5S requires that everyone understand why it is being used and what the expected results are. As with all Lean techniques the aim is improvement in business performance; the adoption is not an end in itself.

Chapter 5: Bringing 5s Home

The 5S system was developed in Japan by Hiroyuki Hirano and was first implemented in the Toyota manufacturing plants in the late 1980's. It is part of the push towards lean manufacturing which emphasizes the elimination of waste. While these principles have been widely adopted by manufactures, they are quite applicable in the home.

Sort (Seiri):
The first step is to eliminate all unnecessary items in a room or space. Get rid of any items that you don't need. If you have any items you are unsure of, red tag them. This involves placing a red tag on any questionable items and placing those items in a designated holding area in a storage room or other out-of-the-way place. Items that remain in the holding area beyond a set time (i.e. three months) will be discarded. Those that are used can be stored in a lower prior location (see next "S" for more details).

Each person will have to modify this system to account for unique needs (i.e. holidays and other seasonal changes), but it is important to avoid the **"just in case"** mentality. The more you are able to get rid of, the easier the next four steps will be and the more likely you will be in successfully maintaining a clean, clutter-free, and organized home.

Set in Order (Seiton):
Once the area is free of unneeded items the area and all remaining items need to be set in order. If any cosmetic

changes, modifications, or repairs need to be made (i.e. painting walls, putting up shelves, etc.), now is a good time to do so.

Once those jobs are done, items need to be organized in a logical way. Because most of us have at least some degree of laziness in us, the better the area is organized, the more likely it is to stay that way. Some questions that need to be addressed include:
- What jobs need to be performed in the area?
- What tools will I need to complete those jobs?
- How often and where exactly in the space will I use each item?
- What are potential safety hazards within the space?

Keeping those questions in mind, find a place for everything. Simply put, everything needs a place, and everything needs to be in its place. Using labels, shadow boards, and other visual cues, designate a place for each item. It needs to be clear where things are so that the system can be maintained by everyone in the home. This will help keep the area clutter-free and make items easy to find.

Shine (Seiso):
Now that unnecessary items are removed, and we have a place for everything that will remain in the space, it is time do clean and polish. Deep clean the space and all items in the space. Take pictures of the space so you know what it can and should look like. Next, set up a cleaning schedule to maintain the cleanliness.

Standardize (Seiketsu):
Standardize the cleaning and maintenance of the area. This can be accomplished with checklists and the schedules and pictures established in the Shine step. The purpose of this step is to ensure the results of the shine step are reproducible by everyone in the house who shares in the cleaning duties. Everyone needs to know what the expectations are and how those expectations can be met.

Sustain (Shitsuke):
Sustaining the system required discipline. Getting everyone to buy into the system is a big part of this step. Soliciting input from family members on how the system is going and how it can be improved will help them get on board and stay on board. If you have put a solid effort into the first four steps and got everyone in the house on board, you are well on your way to a clean and organized home.

Chapter 6: Visual Home/Office and 5s

How organized are you?

The information covered on the next few pages will change your approach to organization forever. Many shows on cable television are based on this thinking, whether they come out and say it or not. What I am talking about is the organizational standards created by Toyota, and now used throughout many companies. In fact, when most companies begin their Lean journey, they start with 5S. Sort, Set-in-Order, Shine, Standardize, and Sustain. Let's start from the top.

Sort

Just as it sounds, you need to pick and choose what you want to keep and what you can get rid of. The main point is that you want to separate the needed items from the unneeded ones. I know I could have used words other than "needed" and "unneeded" but that is the main point of this; keep only what you need!

In manufacturing, a good rule of thumb is the 48 Hour Rule; if you don't need to use it in the next 48 hours, get rid of it, or put it back in its place. This rule works well when organizing a kitchen, garage, or workshop, but you can expand the time frame depending on your particular project. Some people say a month, others 6 months, and some even say years. At any rate, the main thing is; if you don't need it now, and you don't need it soon, statistics say that you probably don't need it at all.

A second good motto to follow is; when in doubt, throw it out! Sort is the hardest step for anyone that is a pack rat. People in my family, I won't say who, have a very hard time getting rid of things. They, like many others, believe that they have something that is salvageable and that someday it will be worth a lot of money. However, for the majority of the items out there, that is not true. Of course, every once in a long while you will find a 1909 baseball card worth $500,000 or maybe even an original copy of the Constitution in the back of an old frame, but chances are, it's worth little to nothing.

To make Sort a little fun and perhaps, even a little fulfilling, try some of these ideas:

- The classic yard/garage sale. This is a great idea because once people see that no one wants to hand over cash for their junk, they are more apt to let go of it. Also, an added bonus is that anything that sells; gets the item out of your hands and gives you some extra spending money!

- Another version of the yard sale is the online auction. Join any of the major auction sites and list as many products as you want. If it sells, then good, you get money and you get rid of it. If not, then you know it's time to throw it away and move on. The only downside is that you will have to pay a small insertion fee up front on most of the sites.

- I like this option the best, because it really allows you to see that if no one in a world of 6,000,000,000+ people wants to buy your stuff, who else is going to be willing to buy it? Get rid of it!

- Give as much of it to charity as you can. The Salvation Army and Good Will Stores always have need for old clothes and household goods. Just make sure they are in good condition. They will also accept children's clothes and toys. The best benefit of this option is that you can claim your donations when you file your taxes for the year in which the items were donated. When you bring items to the donation site, ask one of the employees there for a donation claim form. You fill it out there and they keep a cop and give you one for tax filing. They will also give you a guide that it to be used for estimating the value that you should claim based on the items donated, the total number of items and the overall condition of each item.

- The last creative idea if you have children is to get them involved. They love to help out, and the lesson of letting go will really grow with them as they get older. A lot of American and Western European children have way too many toys as it is. So, an idea here is, explain to them that some children have no toys at all and that they should give a few of their extras to those less fortunate. This will be rewarding, not only for you, but also for your children, as they will learn to share. And all this will contribute towards ridding your house of clutter.

One more thing about Sort – Don't forget to recycle anything that can be re-used!

Set in Order

Now that you have sorted out everything that you no longer need, it's time for Set in order. This step is really the first step towards organization. It covers a broad range of areas, but the message is still the same; arrange items in a set manner so that they are easily accessible, returnable, and at the same time, out of the way. One term that makes it easy to remember is; "A place for everything and everything in its place".

The basic premise is that by arranging things in a logical and accessible manner, you will be more efficient in your actions, and over time, more apt to keep order because it will be evident when something is missing or out of place. Uses for this stretch from a desk in an office to a workshop in the garage to the refrigerator, and even to things like a bathroom or laundry closet. So, now that we have only retained what we actually need, let's arrange it.

There are a few key ways of organizing to use here:

- Common use items (i.e., items used together).
- Arrange by Frequency of Use (i.e., storing items that are used most of the time in an easily accessible space).
- Arrange by Sequence of Use (i.e., storing items in the same sequence as they are used).
- Bulk area that an object occupies.

The first one is pretty self explanatory; arrange items that are commonly used together. In most cases, this is already done. Looking at a house on a macro level, this would be the different areas of the house and what they contain. In the garage or shed, people generally keep tools for upkeep and improvements. This is the same for the kitchen and the bathrooms. On a micro level, you would look at only one of those areas, like the garage. Here you sort it into subgroups; like tools for yard work and tools for housework. That is why grouping commonly used items is usually the first way we arrange things.

Another way is to arrange items by frequency of use. The more you use something, the easier you should be able to retrieve and return it. Just as that sounds, you want to store things so that they are more accessible than other not-so-frequently-used items. Some good examples of this; in a bathroom, you use hand soap every time you visit, but you only use the shower/toilet cleanser once a week, so you did store the hand soap on the sink and the cleanser in a closet or cabinet somewhere within the bathroom. Working in your garage, you use your hammer and screwdrivers for 80% of your jobs and your jigsaw for only 20%. Same deal here, you did store your hammer and screwdrivers easily within reach, while the jigsaw would lie tucked neatly away in its own home until you need it.

Does this sound like common sense? Well, it is, but too many times people forget the power of organization. Okay, back to the organizing.

The next way to store is by sequence of use. This may sound like storing things that are commonly used together, but it is not quite the same thing. This takes it all one step further. While
It is true that most of these items are used together; the sequence they are used in is the driving force in their storage. A basic example from manufacturing that I can use to describe this would be working on a hamburger assembly line that makes

burgers with lettuce, tomato, and ketchup. So, if the work goes from left to right, you did store these items in this sequence, left to right; bottom half of the bun, hamburger patty, lettuce, tomato, ketchup, and finally, the top bun. That example may seem a little too simple, but it gets my point across. Again, there are so many different cases in which you can apply this method.

Finally, another way to store things is by the bulk area an object occupies. The bigger something is, the harder it will be to store in one of the previous methods. For anything like this, simply create a home for it and store it there. Common examples are lawn mowers, laundry baskets, kitchen appliances, large mixing bowls, etc.

Now, we have learned how to store in order, let's learn how to give everything its own home. Some common methods for creating "homes" include:
- Labelling
- Outlining
- Colour Coding

I really take labelling to the extreme. Everywhere that I have worked, I was required to "5S" my desk. Because of this, I had labels everywhere! And because of that, I was able to stay organized. If you look at my desk you'd see labels that said, "stapler", "calculator", "notepad", etc. Now, when I tell people this, they generally give me a weird look and don't understand why anyone would do this. And many other people in the office often felt this way as well until they started working at their newly "5S'd" desk. That doubt quickly turns around, and many can't go home at night until they find their missing stapler.

Let's get started, here are some tips for Labelling:

- Use a label maker: it is much neater than hand writing and provides labels that are easy to remove.
- If possible, put a label on the item itself and on also on the spot that it occupies. If it is missing, you will know instantly and if someone else finds it, they will know where to return it.

A second way of creating "homes" for objects is thru the use of outlining or shadow boarding. This is primarily affective in areas that you can use paint or permanent marker. A good, real world example includes the use of lines to create parking spaces. An at home use is generally done in a home workshop (but can also be done with utensils and items in the kitchen). This would be your typical shadow board. Basically, tools are hung on a pegboard or wall and then either outlined or the shape of the object is painted on the board. So, if you remove the hammer, you did see either an outline of a hammer or a silhouette of one. If it is missing, it will be very evident.

Another good way to practice Set-in-Order is colour coding. You can use colour coding throughout your house, office, tool shed, etc. Some people consider this part of the 4th S (Standardize), but it really fits in well for both steps. Colour coding really gets things organized because it is one of the only ways to make something visually distinguishable, which again is that Visual Factory aspect of Lean.

Some people think that I am crazy when I suggest colour coding certain things, but we grow up surrounded by colours telling what's what. For example in the US, stop lights, green means go, red means stop, and yellow means slow down or in the UK get ready to stop or ready to go. Red is usually a sign of a problem or warning. At any diner in the U.S., decaf coffee is poured from the orange rimmed pot, while regular coffee comes out of the black (sometimes brown) rimmed one. And my favourite example, casino checks/chips. Throughout the gaming industry, casinos generally use the following colour code: $1 chips are white (or blue), $5 chips are red, $25 are green, $100 chips are black, $500 chips are purple, and $1,000 chips are orange. Then they add more colours on the edges to help indicate how many are stacked together. With these edge spots, they can also look down from any camera in the casino to see if someone was paid too much or not enough, and in some cases, they use these spots to prevent cheating and quickly identify losses due to cheating. From the examples I've just shown, colour coding has a reach, far beyond manufacturing facilities.

In industry, colour coding is usually used to distinguish one production line's tools and materials from another. Here each area, line or cell will be given its own colour. Tools, jigs and dies will be the same colour as the area it is used in. So, if another area loses a tool, it can be found and easily identified by any other area. This also comes in handy when workers tend to take each other's tools. No one wants to be working in an area with red machinery and tools, and be using a yellow wrench. Anyone can see from a distance that this tool does not belong to them and that they have obviously gone against policy and stolen someone else's tool. This same concept can be really affective if applied in a home.

For anyone that has multiple children, you will find this particularly useful. Assign children a certain colour that they use to identify themselves but be sure that you let them pick it! (If you have more than one child that wants the same colour, ask them to give a second choice that can be used as a minor colour. E.g., John and Jim both want yellow. John also likes grey, while Jim like black. So, here you could give John yellow with a grey stripe, and Jim can be yellow with a black stripe).

I know you might be thinking that this seems crazy, but for younger children it really helps them identify their own things and take care of them, while at the same time they learn to respect the belongings of others. Common things to try this with: tooth brushes, lunch boxes, toys, tools, clothes, etc. Remember, most children like the fact that they have their own colour and that they picked it, so many see this as a game rather than a way of keeping them organized.

Aside from children, colour coding works well for most household areas. Some items are already colour coded when you get them, like salt and pepper shakers that you use in the kitchen. Here are some basic ideas to get you oriented with colour coding:

- For chemicals, like cleaners: Use bright coloured stickers such as red or green to indicate very harmful ones from lighter, safer chemicals. You can also use a simple colour sticker to represent any products with bleach or ammonia. Make chemicals that react strongly together have two different labels, and create a small reference chart to remind everyone to not, for example, mix the red and green ones.

- Stickers in the kitchen can tell you about the seasoning or taste of something. I like to use this on wine bottles. If you think about salsa containers; they have green for Mild, yellow for Medium, and red for Hot. Well, I do the same thing for wine that I store in my house. After opening and tasting the first bottle of a case, I am able to put a sticker on the back of the bottle that depending on the colour, reminds me that this has a "smooth, mellow" taste or a "spicy, dry" finish, etc.

- Create a schedule for sticker colours to use in the fridge and cupboards. I like to put 8 different stickers on the items in my refrigerator and cupboards. Items in the cupboard get a date within that sticker as well. Each sticker is a different colour and represents a different week over two months. I do this so that when I go to use something in the refrigerator, I know whether it is good or bad. I have a tendency to leave things around and they go bad. When I started doing this, I was able to not play the guessing game and keep my refrigerator only filled with items that are still edible. You can put a date on the sticker if that helps you too, but the main thing is still that it enables you to identify the good items vs. the bad items.

More and more companies are using colour coding outside of their plants as well. Most notably, within the past few years, has recreated the prescription pill bottle. I have always said that they "5S'd" it, since they looked at it from a customer standpoint, took out the waste and put in more value added features. They improved the human factor side of the product and most customers responded favourably. Each family member is given a colour, so that each bottle is distinguishable by sight, they have made the font bigger, more organized and detailed, but still readable, drug facts and warnings.

Another good use of colour is from the computer and consumer electronics industry. All of the components that connect to the back of the computer are colour coded so that the peripheral connector matches the connector on the computer. Some people said it was brilliant. I just say it's simple, common sense.

Shine

The 3rd "S" is really something simple. **Shine:** All this means is to clean up and make things sparkle or shine. This is sometimes referred to as Spick and Span as well. The point is the same, however, once we have Sorted and Set-in-order, it is time to clean up what is left. During Shine, there are three main goals.
- Getting the area or workplace clean.
- Maintaining its appearance.
- Installing and using preventive measures to keep it that way.

Here are some common practices to help achieve this:

- Painting
- Lighting
- Removing clutter
- Dust collection
- Minimizing leaks and spills.
- Conducting routing maintenance (i.e., preventive maintenance).
- Use of root cause analysis.

There are many more that I could list, but you get the point. CLEAN UP!

Standardize

After cleaning your separated items, it is now time to standardize everything. Standardize can be done in a variety of ways, which will include some of the Set-in-order process like colour coding and visual identification practices. In industry, Standardize is used to make the 1st 3 S's "unbreakable" by installing a system of standards that is to be followed by everyone within the organization. This is where roles and responsibilities are handed out and training occurs to get everyone used to the 5S vocabulary. Also, a lot of emphasis is put towards the use of visual factory techniques; colour coding, checklists, and labelling that reinforce a "copy as you see it" approach. In a home or office, the same techniques and approach work well.

Here are some strategies to get to standardization:

1. Use 5WHYs and 1 HOW – Keep asking WHY until you get to the root cause and then ask HOW to fix it. Some very basic examples:

Industry:
- o WHY are you spending half your day mopping the floor?
- Answer: Because oil is always leaking from the machine.

- WHY is oil leaking from the machine?
- Answer: The secondary gasket isn't strong enough to hold the oil.

- WHY isn't it strong enough?
- Answer: The primary gasket is missing.

- WHY hasn't it been replaced?
- Answer: The maintenance department can't get the screw off.

- WHY can't they get the screw off?
- Answer: They don't have the right tool.

- HOW: I will have them order the proper tool, and replace it.

Lifestyle:
- WHY have I gained 20 pounds in the past year?
- Answer: Because I eat too many bad foods.

- WHY do I eat at bad foods when I shouldn't?
- Answer: Because I don't have time to prepare and eat well.

- WHY don't I have time?
- Answer: I get up late every morning and need to rush.

- WHY do I get up so late every morning?
- Answer: I don't get to sleep until the early morning.

- WHY don't I get to sleep until then?

- Answer: I stay up watching late night television.
  ○ HOW: Ignore (or record) late night television and go to sleep.

2. Suspension of toys, food, tools, etc: When people forget or ignore the 1st 3 S's that you have installed, punish them this way so that over time, the system is reinforced and eventually sustained.

3. Incorporate Poka-yokes (this is talked about in depth in another section) – means "error-proofing" some examples: locks on chemical cabinets, used of baby or puppy gates, putting things out of reach, etc.

4. Eliminate as many variations as possible, examples:
- Tool unification – use only Phillips head screws and screwdrivers on all home projects.
- Tool substitution – wing nuts instead of wrench turned bolts.
- Method substitution – eliminate the bolts and use clamps (many areas where this can apply especially workshops or the kitchen)

Sustain

Of the 5S's, Sustain is by far the hardest to fully accomplish; partly because it is a never ending process of ongoing improvement, but mostly because it requires constant monitoring of the first 4S's. In manufacturing, it is relatively simple because you can reward or punish certain people or work areas, while at home, it may involve only you, which in turn, requires much more self discipline and control. Regardless of the troubles, here is how you keep it going:

- If you have children or others that are living or working in a 5S'd environment (e.g., your newly cleaned/organized kitchen), let them know beforehand that they will be required to keep it neat and orderly. If you were able to Standardize well, then they will already have good tools to use in order to Sustain.

- Perform audits. This lets anyone involved know where they stand and what needs to be improved. Auditing yourself can be tough, but it does provide you with how well you have been able to keep it up.

- Take pictures of the area at its cleanest point and then put them in the area. This has the effect of putting a "fat" picture of yourself on the refrigerator when you want to discourage yourself from eating.

- Use checklists daily, weekly, whatever is most suitable for you.

- Assign yourself and others involved tasks to be completed on a scheduled basis. Reprimand when they have not been completed and give acknowledgement once completed.

- Do as much as you can to keep it going: signs, pictures, reminders, notes, etc. Make the awareness remain at a very high level of visibility.

Additional Esses!

Three other phases are sometimes included: safety, security, and satisfaction. This is however not a traditional set of "phases". Safety for example is inherent in the 5S methodology and is not a step in itself. Therefore the additions of the phases are simply to clarify the benefits of 5S and not a different or more inclusive methodology.

Safety

A sixth phase, "Safety", is sometimes added. There is debate over whether including this sixth "S" promotes safety by stating this value explicitly, or if a comprehensive safety program is undermined when it is relegated to a single item in an efficiency-focused business methodology.

Security

A seventh phase, "Security", can also be added. To leverage security as an investment rather than an expense, the seventh "S" identifies and addresses risks to key business categories including fixed assets, material, human capital, brand equity, intellectual property, information technology, assets-in-transit and the extended supply chain.

Satisfaction

An eighth phase, "Satisfaction", can be included. Employee Satisfaction and engagement in continuous improvement activities ensures the improvements will be sustained and improved upon. The Eighth waste Non Utilized Intellect, Talent, and Resources can be the most damaging waste of all.

It is important to have continuous education about maintaining standards. When there are changes that affect the 5S program such as new equipment, new products or new work rules, it is essential to make changes in the standards and provide training. Companies embracing 5S often use posters and signs as a way of educating employees and maintaining standards.

Chapter 7: 5S Housekeeping at Home

Do you find following things within fifteen to twenty seconds in your home when they are needed?

- A particular medicine; say antacid tablets, pain killers, your daily medicines doctor prescribed, sprain cream etc.
- Postage and related material: say stamps, envelops, inland letters, post cards, glue, gem clips, stapler, staple pins, stationery etc.
- Bank documents; like pay-in-slips, check books etc.
- Income tax related documents; like papers related to your investments, previous years' income tax returns etc.
- Electricity/power bills, telephone bills, water bills, corporation tax bills etc.
- Telephone numbers and addresses of your particular relative or friend or your or your spouse's particular colleague.
- Writing pad and pen/pencil to take down the messages over the telephone.
- Locks and keys of your house, scooters, car(s), cupboards, safe deposit lockers, office, the keys and locks of your suitcases, brief cases etc.
- Desired pair of shoes/footwear, matching clothes, hairpins, kerchief, nail polish, lip stick etc.
- Children's school bag, books, notebooks, their shoes/footwear, socks, progress cards, i-cards, date of

- birth certificate, their particular toys, ink bottles, pens, pencils etc.
- The stitching kit like pairs of scissors, sewing needles, threads of particular colours and types, buttons of various types, measuring tape, knives etc.
- Towels, toothpaste, tooth brushes, soaps, detergents.
- Candles and match box when the light/power goes off suddenly.
- The tong, the gas lighter, the hand mixer, right kind of serving bowls, right kind of cutlery, cups and saucers.
- The cooking recipes you so diligently took down from a TV program, or copied from a magazine or web site.
- A particular novel or book/magazine you wish to read today, now.
- Your housecoat when suddenly some guests arrive and you have to receive them at your door.
- The money or change you kept somewhere.
- Yours or your spouse's i-cards, credit cards, passports, club membership cards etc.
- Shoe polish of various colours and types, shoe brushes, shoe laces etc.

If your answers to many of these questions and such other possible questions are in negative or you have hesitation in answering them, you have large scope of improving your housekeeping following the 5S Housekeeping steps in this book.

Did Any of the Following Things Happen at Your Home at Least Once in the Past Six Months or One Year?
- Your kitchen or other rooms of the house got flooded with water since somebody in the house kept the taps open.

- Electricity/power bill suddenly shot up during some months because the family members are not in the habit of not switching off the air-conditioners, heaters, lights, fans, geysers/boilers, ovens, computers and other electrical appliances when not in use.
- The sauce/ketchup, pickles, jam, shampoo, oil bottles' caps were not securely placed and so got dropped and broke and the contents were wasted.
- The computer, printer, mixer, fans, clocks/watches etc stopped working suddenly as too much of dirt and dust jammed the inside of these machines and you had to pay heavily to get them rectified that too not to your satisfaction or you had to buy the new ones with lots of extra expenditure not planned.
- You had to buy an additional cupboard (storage space) or two to store the things because the existing storage space had fully been utilized.
- You found cockroaches and spiders etc many times in your utensils, cups and saucers and in many others items at your home.
- You or any other member(s) of the family was injured by the shaving blade which was used up but not disposed off and was rusted.
- Did you find rusted hair clips, rusted safety pins lying on the wash basins of your home and the rust spoiling the wash basin and also the possibility of using these rusted items by you or the members of your family?
- Your bath room was not dry and as slippery and as a result someone slipped off, fell down and got injured or got electric shock due to wet floor (if he/she was an old person, it can be very dangerous).

If your answer to many of these questions is in affirmation, you need to consider giving 5S Housekeeping a high priority for your home.

A large number of home makers wish to be efficient. And they should be. Why not? They wish to hurry up everything because of lack of time and compulsions of punctuality for every activity.

Then, for accomplishing it, they take out everything that is needed to finish up that job within the time available. For example, take cooking. You have pressure on you of completing the cooking in time since you, your spouse and children have to start for their work places on time. You pick out from the cupboards all the needed utensils, all the gadgets, all the raw materials and spread all of them around you, all at a time on your kitchen platform and island thinking that placing everything around you would allow you easy access to them. But the very clutter around you really becomes an obstacle in efficient working. Plus, you are compromising on safety due to the clutter. It looks untidy and loses aesthetics.

After the cooking is complete, you find that there are hundred things on your kitchen platform and island now and you just do not have time and energy to put these things back in the places meant for them. It's time up for you; you and everyone else in the family have to rush out to accomplish the next tasks ahead. So, you leave the kitchen in this kind of unorganized condition. Then, in the evening, you start from where you left, take out some more things to do the evening's cooking and the clutter keeps mounting. The whole of kitchen starts looking untidy. The retrieval is difficult and time consuming. It's unsafe.

Rather than doing this, plan out your cooking sequence. Take out one thing at a time from the cupboards that are just a step away from you in the kitchen; they are not far away from you. After you have used that thing, put it back in the cupboard in its place immediately. The time taken to use that item is the same- you are not taking any extra time or losing any time. You are as efficient. Do this for each item of use. Take it out, use it and place it back in the same condition in which you took it (if there was a lid on bottle, place it back securely) and position it in the same place from where you took it out.

You will take same amount of time and there would not be any clutter around. The kitchen will look tidy and will be a safe place to work.

Give it a try.

Benefits of Adopting 5S Housekeeping at Home

- Home looks clean, tidy and beautiful.
- Feels great to live in such a home.
- Impresses everyone.
- Improves hygiene at home.
- No one at home wastes any time in searching and retrieving the things.
- Home is a safe place now.
- The environment around is clean and healthy.
- There is no clutter around.
- You don't need to spend money to procure additional storage space or equipment for that clutter (had you not done the 5S Housekeeping, the clutter would have increased). So, you are saving lots of money.

You will experience more and more surprising advantages as you start implementing 5S Housekeeping at home.

Chapter 8: Ways to Kill Clutter in 5 Minutes

My son once said; "one of the biggest reasons for the pervasive clutter in my apartment is lack of time to deal with it. It takes longer to put a shirt away than it does to just throw it on the floor, so onto the floor it goes. As long as there's a path from the door to my bed, I tend not to ignore and perpetuate the clutter. I'm increasingly realizing, though, that all the out-of-place stuff in my life can become a huge time drain. I spend precious minutes and hours looking for things that could be easily avoided by a better system, and a few minutes devoted to staying organized."

In an effort to get him more organized, especially in his personal space, I showed him few methods that can help even the busiest of us to get organized, or at least get the organization ball rolling, in only a few minutes. In the time it takes to brush his teeth or check his voicemail, I am able to get some of the junk in his life a little more in order.

Here are eight ways to get in, get organized, and get out.

1. Between the shelves, the desks, the drawers, the nooks and the crannies, the things you need to deal with get pretty spread out. To tackle them, try the "One Box" method; take out a box, as large as possible, and put everything you need to deal with into it. Clear the junk off of every surface, and if you need to do something with it, don't just put it in the box. It's much easier to sit

down later with a box and dig into processing it, than it is to try to clean and organize all at once. I call it the "Box of Everything," and it will make your space cleaner and give you an easier time of processing the relevant stuff. When in doubt, put it in the box.

2. Pick a single space in your room or office, a desk, a bookshelf, a chair piled with laundry and clean it until it's spic-and-span. Make sure it's a small space, as you are trying to get this done in five minutes, but pick a spot and have a mini-cleaning bonanza. Most small spaces will only have a few items to deal with, which will make the process both easy and rewarding, as at least one small part of your mess looks immaculate.

3. Do a sweep of your whole space; office, bedroom, wherever you are looking to get organized. Anything that needs to be processed or dealt with separately, leave where it is. For these five minutes, all you are dealing with is trash-able items. Walk around with a big trash bag, and liberally dump stuff into it. I find that a huge portion of the clutter in my own room is due to things I meant to throw away, but for whatever reason didn't before now. In five minutes, you'll fill a trash bag and make your space look that much nicer.

4. In most rooms, a dirty or cluttered floor is the most obvious sign of disorganization. There is significant psychological benefit in a clean floor, and it's much easier to keep the floor clean if it's clean to begin with. Try cleaning just the floor if something's not touching the floor, leave it alone. Most of what is on my son's

floor are clothes, shoes, and other things; he have the terrible tendency to walk into his room, drop, and walk back out. With a clean floor, your space will look better and feel better to you, and likely make the task of organizing much less daunting.

5. Another thing prone to messing up your space is things without a home. The easiest way to fix this? Give them a home. Start by picking a place for all of a certain thing to go let's say DVDs. Once you have created a home for your DVDs, go around collecting them and putting them in their rightful place. Don't deal with anything else except your DVDs. In just a few minutes, you can collect all your DVDs, put them where they are supposed to be, and be done with it. Organizing your DVDs or whatever it may be gets a whole lot easier when they have a set home and a home only for them.

6. This one's somewhat the opposite of a lot of what I've mentioned, but can work for you depending on your mood. Sometimes, all you want to do is make a mess so large you don't have a choice but to clean it up. When you are feeling this way, you dig everything out of the clever places you tend to hide things; drawers, behind and on top of other things, under your bed, and what have you. Once everything is out, on the floor, and in front of you, you are able to gauge what it is that you are dealing with, and get to work. If you are not in the mood to clean, but know you should, try this one; make the mess messier, but in a useful way.

7. Organizing is simply more fun when there is a flashy, cool system to it. That is why I always suggested the use of a labeller for your filing system; it is no more useful than a pen, and probably takes longer, but it is prettier and more serious-looking. This is a great tip for when you don't want to clean up at all; make some files. Figure out what you've got a lot of, and create a file for it. Make it pretty, easy to get to, and I've found they tend to fill themselves up somehow.

8. This is a new habit, and it's worked wonders for me. When I'm organizing, I put duct tape over certain places; my bookshelf and my cupboard, for instance. They are off-limits, and I'm not allowed to put things in them. Now, instead of being able to just shove things in drawers and hope for an "out of sight, out of mind" mentality, I have to find a useful place for them or just get rid of them. Mostly, it's just get rid of them. I leave myself a finite amount of space for my things, and it's typically easy to shrink my stuff to fill the space.

Organizing works best in baby steps- trying to do it all at once can be overwhelming. Instead, take five minutes, and tackle one of these eight tasks; you will feel better, your space will look better, and organization will somehow begin to look a little bit easier.

Chapter 9: 5s Bedroom

I have struggled with keeping my bedroom clean for my entire life. When I was younger, it just wasn't important and now it seems that it ends up being the catch-all for dirty and clean laundry, dog toys and other random assorted things that get set down during the day. Well today I say "enough is enough" as I implement these 5 steps into my cleaning routine!

1. Change the Sheets: There is just something about a freshly made bed that reminds me of my mother. It's like a linen-filled guilt trip that instantly makes the rest of the room more dirty and shameful. By starting here you are willing yourself to make everything else in the space amazing to live up to the crisp, clean standard that sheets set.

2. Everything has its place: One of the most difficult assaults that our bedroom undergoes is the constant struggle for everything to find its place. It is been admittedly more difficult since a recent move and so things have been slightly in upheaval but by making sure all the little things have a home, ensures they are not on your floor or furniture. Make a list of everything that hits the floor or top of your dresser for a week and work on creating a solid home for those things. Belts beware, you are about to get a permanent home so I will quit stepping on you in the middle of the night!

3. Surface clean day: It's easy to forget about cleaning the surfaces in your bedroom. Schedule time during your week to wipe down electronics, furniture, windowsills and mirrors. When you do it each week instead of once a year, it can happen

on commercial break while watching Top Chef even (though there is actually enough commercials on Bravo to clean your entire house by!). Done!

4. Pick up after Pets: In our house we have two dogs. One sleeps in her own dog bed, the other dives under the covers with us. It's easy to assume that as long as one of them isn't yacking up dinner that there isn't much to clean up after. They are easy-going laid back type dogs that don't require much maintenance; but the more I looked, the more I was wrong. I know my bedroom would be a healthier place if I took the time to vacuum the sheets, dog bed and floors every other day like I do my sofa (for the same reason). It would also help pick up the stray fluff from gutted toys. My bedroom isn't a dog cave, but things would stay fresher longer if this was implemented.

5. Thin Down, Throw It Out, Donate It Away: It's easy to accumulate clothes, shoes, and accessories you are not 100% in love with. If you don't tailor your clothes then quite often you find yourself struggling to find things that fit just right. Often pieces in your closet will be a little short, a little funky, a little tight, a little baggy, a little "something" that makes you not 100% in love with them. Get them out, thin out what you have and let the things you love shine. You'll always be happy to get dressed and have less to put away or hang up. Our bedroom is extra guilty of this, but "enough is enough" and we are headed to the thrift store this weekend!

Chapter 10: Kitchens Are Already Lean

Most kitchens are already arranged around some lean principles.

Small Batches
People don't make hundreds of meals at a time and only eat the first meal after the final meal has finished production. They make one meal at a time and eat it immediately.

Work Cells
In kitchens with a good work flow, the food flows from one station to the next (fridge, counter, stove, table) in a smooth progression. The tools are arranged by where they are needed in the flow of cooking rather than by their function. For example, the microwave and the stove aren't always next to each other just because they are both "ovens," they are placed wherever they might be used in the process.

Small inventories
With the exception of people buying in bulk, it is not traditional for families to purchase a full year's groceries at a time and then store it. They buy what they need for a week or two at most, then use it up quickly. There's no need (and usually not much room) for huge inventories.

No wasted motion or transportation
A well-arranged kitchen will have the appliances arranged in a convenient triangle pattern so there is only a step or two needed to get a plate anywhere in the kitchen.

Right-sized equipment
The stove or blender is big enough for the family's needs, but small enough that maintenance and upkeep are minimized.

Unfortunately, these observations are only true for "well-arranged kitchens." Many kitchens are poorly arranged, with wasted space, counter-productive layouts and little difficult-to-reach storage areas where items can go hiding.

Our kitchen, for instance, is not laid out in the most functional pattern possible simply because the architecture won't allow it. (This is true for most people who don't design their own kitchens as a friend of mine did.) There are five doors and two windows, which severely limit arrangement options along the limited wall space.

Even when you can design your own kitchen with lean production in mind, it is easy to veer off track as impressing people can be almost as important as getting things done. Modern dream kitchens, with their huge floorplans, massive central islands and huge rows of cabinetry, will inevitably be cursed with large amounts of wasted motion, an over-accumulation of inventory, and an over-sizing of common tools (e.g., using a massive professional stove for a small family's cooking needs).

So are most kitchens lean by nature? No. In fact, I'd guess that very few of them are, even in the best of circumstances. But they can all get leaner, even in the worst of circumstances. Our kitchen is proof of that.

Chapter 11: Attacking the Kitchen With 5s

I did prefer to jump right in and start stripping out waste, but looking at the kitchen I realize we are not ready for that. Before we get into streamlining, we will need to get the place organized better. There is too much clutter to even see where the subtle kinds of waste might be.

This isn't uncommon; many flowcharts of lean transformations that I have seen include a cleaning-and-reorganizing step before you get into the core work of lean improvements.

But there is a hitch: If you don't know how you are going to be organizing the lean process that you are putting in place after the spring-cleaning, how can you really clean and reorganize things without wasting a lot of time? That is, if the final goal is unclear, how can you really work towards it?

My view is that what our kitchen needs right now is to give us the simple ability to see what is there. Once everything is visible and at least arranged so similar items are close together, it will be more obvious what we are dealing with when the real organizing begins.

Are your kitchen ingredients labelled for 5S efficiency?

Every so often I think of a quality improvement technique that might help me when I am home cleaning and organizing, or doing some of my other house duties.

A 5S audit is a quality improvement technique developed to standardize a workplace for effectiveness by tracking the results of the following 5 phases: sort, set in order, shine, standardize, and sustain. It is really the perfect tool for keeping an organized kitchen. And believe me; I am no Top Chef, but 5S helps me keep my kitchen in order!

Sort

Ask yourself: Are all the items involved really necessary? Here is your chance to get rid of that broken hand blender and throw away the three extra discoloured spatulas you have hanging around. Do you rarely use that wine chiller that is taking up precious counter space? Put all kitchen gadgets you use only occasionally in a pantry closet, reserving counter space for the kitchen appliances you use most.

Set in Order

Ask yourself: Is each kitchen tool close to where it will be used? Are items clearly labelled? To prevent the salt-instead-of-sugar problem when making a pumpkin pie, clearly label ingredients if you have them kept in countertop canisters. I realized I was keeping dishwashing detergent in the hallway pantry, rather than in the cabinet right next to the dishwasher.

Keep your flow path simplified to optimize the time you spend preparing foods by finding all the ingredients you need for a recipe before you begin. This can also help you prevent those last-minute trips to the grocery store.

Shine

Keeping your kitchen clean: After cooking, it can be tempting to leave the pile of dishes in the sink and wash them later. It is important to tackle these messes as you cook. If you have downtime waiting for something to finish cooking, load the dishwasher or wipe off a messy countertop. This will drastically decrease your clean up time after cooking. Leaving your kitchen untidy for several days could increase your chances for food borne illnesses! And in the case of a factory, a messy workspace can hide signs that equipment or process steps are malfunctioning.

Standardize

Is everyone in your family aware of standard kitchen procedures?

My wife will love this one. Does everyone know the optimal way to load a dishwasher so that the most dishes can be loaded and cleaned correctly? And in the case of manufacturing, keeping procedures correctly documented and work stations identical will help keep duties standardized.

Sustain

Can these standards be maintained? Are your kitchen tools being stored in their correct places? Are you always thinking of new and better ways of completing a process or using a new tool?

While these questions can help you eliminate wasteful behaviour in your kitchen, they were originally developed to help you improve processes within your job and your company. Taking note of these considerations (on paper and discussing in meetings) can help you get organized and improve productivity.

In my attempt to get our kitchen prepared for leaner cooking, I began the famous 5S workplace-organization process that usually kicks off lean transformations. The idea is that once you get your workspace organized, you can really start finding the wastes in your process. Naturally, as you uncover and eliminate waste, you will do further reorganizing. So the 5S process is just a systematic method for hitting a moving target wherever it is right now, not something set in stone.

The first S in the "5 S's" is commonly translated in English as "Sort." That translation doesn't quite capture the intended meaning, as the Japanese word "seiri" means something more like "Disposition." But fans of the 5S's, enjoying how all of the step names began with an S in Japanese, have tolerated some clumsy translating to make them all begin with S in English, too. That's okay, Sort works just fine.

Anyway, the Sort step involves going through the workspace and getting rid of anything that doesn't contribute to the work being done. One method, as described earlier in this book to red tag anything that might be superfluous and move it to a separate staging area where supervisors can look through it. The goal is to store, transfer, or eliminate anything in the workspace that doesn't help or even worse, gets in the way of the work being done.

I have designated as our red-tag staging ground one end of our dining room table. I will be moving everything there that doesn't really seem helpful in the kitchen, awaiting a decision on what to do with it.

It is hard to know what is truly necessary in a kitchen because unlike a factory, a kitchen is both a workspace and a living space. Some things in a kitchen are there purely for aesthetic appeal even though they aren't really helpful in the act of cooking. What really deserves to get the boot?

For now I am going with the simple rule that aesthetic objects are fine, but only if they don't get in the way of creating a good cooking space. So wall hangings, yes. Decorative jars that take up counter space, no.

Speaking of decorative jars, we have a set of large vintage glass jars on our kitchen counter that we have long envisioned holding cookies and other treats for our little kids. The problem is that the kids are still too young for such things, so the jars have instead become random bric-a-brac containers that take up a lot of counter space without adding to the cooking process at all.

I did been wracking my brain trying to figure out how to repurpose those jars, because among other things, I assumed my wife would never let me move them. When I mentioned this to her, to my surprise she immediately suggested we put them somewhere else. She recognizes that the cookie-jar plans are on hold for now, and wants to make sure the jars don't get broken while pointlessly taking up space on the counters.

I had no idea she felt this way, and never would have if I hadn't mentioned it to her. This reminded me again of a big lesson from lean production:

Most of the change has to come from the bottom up, not from the top down, so involve EVERYBODY in the process of change.

I will try to remember that as I move unneeded items to the staging area over the next few days. It pains me to make the dining room messier just to make the kitchen cleaner, but the dining room has a date with 5S in its future, too...

I continue the process of Sorting in my kitchen. Sorting, the first step of the 5S organization process that kicks off many lean initiatives focuses on getting rid of anything that doesn't support the work you are doing.

In the kitchen, this means getting rid of everything that doesn't support the act of cooking food (which includes decorative elements if they get in the way). I still have a long way to go in this Sorting project; it is amazing how much clutter a kitchen will begin to accumulate. Here are the types of things I am moving to our staging area for removal from the kitchen.

- Non-cooking items. The kitchen includes the heavily-used back door of our house, which means that lots of small items get left on the counters as we pass through on the way into or out of the house. Most of these things have nothing to do with cooking, such as random coupons, correspondence, and other documents, plus car keys and many other items that belong somewhere else.

- Seldom-used cooking items. This includes a coffeemaker that we only use for overnight guests, a heavy cast-iron gingerbread-house pan, which would get used at most once a year and actually has never been used yet. These things clutter up the kitchen and get in the way of everyday cooking.

One reason why the Sorting step is so helpful is that it's often hard to see things until you move them. After I moved a bunch of things to the staging area, both my wife and I noticed how OPEN and AVAILABLE the counters suddenly seemed. We hadn't realized how confined and useless the counters had begun to feel with all the random stuff there was sitting around on them, because the stuff had become invisible to us. Human beings can get used to anything.

This suggests to me another possible lean lesson: Lean techniques require you to continuously work on improving your processes, even after you think the work is already done. Since it can be hard to see how you might further improve a process you have become happy with, it's often necessary to find ways to disrupt your perceptions of the process, temporarily, so you can see it with fresh eyes.

This could involve leveraging a crisis that appears on its own, or it could involve using a systematic problem-evaluation mechanism like the "Five Whys" to make you look deeper than you otherwise might. It could also involve collecting objective data, perhaps numeric, to give you a different take on things. Or as in our case, it might involve moving all of the kitchen counter items to another room before bringing them back in, one by one, so you can think about them outside of their normal context.

Enough writing for now, and more sorting…

As a first step towards "lean" cooking, I am working through the 5S workplace-organization process that begins many lean transformations. I have now completed the First S – "Sorting", in which you toss all the unnecessary stuff and keep only the things you really need at hand to get the task done.

In the course of doing this sorting, I have learned a few things:

You have to be clear on your focus for the space. In the case of the kitchen, the main focus is "preparing meals." There are many other secondary activities that people do in the kitchen, such as socializing, doing odd household jobs, etc., but allowing too much vagueness about what the room was for is what made it cluttered. When it's decision time, I decided that the room was for cooking, period.

You also have to be realistic. Even though our kitchen is for cooking, it's where our back door is, so there needs to be a place to put coats and shoes. By the same token, ours is a nice kitchen, but it does not have dozens of extra cabinets and acres of extra counter space. Some things that we did rather move out have to stay, and some things we did rather stay have to move out. It is a shame, but it is also one of the ways that everyday life is different from a factory: We don't have the luxury of building custom spaces for every task we do.

You may surprise yourself. As I mentioned before, once we moved items from our counters to the staging area on the dining room table, we suddenly realized how unnecessary some previously-critical items were. Now that the counters are wide open and clear, we are reluctant to put things back on them again. So the popcorn popper that just had to be out all the time is finally making the move to a closet after two years on the stove.

Now that the necessary has been separated from the unnecessary, we move on to the next S in the 'Five S's': "Set in order" This step is also sometimes called "Straightening" or "Stabilizing" or "Setting Up" or something like that. (Again, these multiple variations are the consequence of trying to capture the meaning of a Japanese word beginning with S (seiton) with an English word ALSO beginning with S.)

The basic idea of "Set in order" is to put the items in your workspace (which are by now only the truly necessary items for your task) in order. The goal is for the location of items to be efficient, tidy, and easily-understood. Among the commonly mentioned methods:

Let the worker who does the job organize their tools rather than some supervisor. Only the worker knows the right placement for their actual workflow.
Use ample labelling so that anybody attempting to perform the task, even if it's not usually their workspace, can easily find what they need.

Use visual inventory methods, like drawing an outline around the spot where the tool is kept, so it will immediately be clear where something goes (and more important, when something is missing or out of place).

Keep the focus on the work flow. It is more important that a tool be where it needs to be when it is required than making sure it is grouped with similar tools. For instance, wooden spoons need to be near the stove so they can be easily used to stir something in a cooking pot. Sure, wooden spoons could be kept with the dining and serving spoons (since they are all spoons) in a drawer over by the dining room, but that would be valuing "similarity" over "making it easier to cook." Don't worry about external categories, worry about keeping the work flowing.

Enough talk, I'm off to do some set in order.

Chapter 12: Kaizen Versus Kaizen Blitzes

It's been a while since I wrote the previous chapters of this book an update on my applying the "5S" organization process to our kitchen. The reason for this delay is related to something I mentioned once before: We have very little time to do anything but childcare, and definitely don't have big blocks of time to get anything major done without interruption.

I did not realize this would affect the 5S process, but I should have. All of the narratives I have read where companies applied the 5S process to their workspaces took place during big lean rollout workshops. That is, the workers had hours or days totally unobstructed in which to do the full 5S process to its conclusion.

In our household, there is no time for a hiatus or seminar or workshop to get these big changes made. The toddlers are almost always here, and if they aren't here, we aren't either. If something can't be rolled into the daily routine of keeping things going, it can't happen.

So after I Sorted and Set the kitchen in order, the 5S process ground to a halt. There simply isn't the time to do the Sorting and set in order that needs to be done to get it "right." We don't have time to totally go through the cabinets and fridge and freezer and get everything sorted out properly. Despairing of this reality, I got stuck.

There is a bigger issue here: At the centre of lean production is the concept of kaizen, meaning "continuous incremental improvement." The idea is that the lean worker is always looking for ways to improve the process, even in tiny ways, in a cycle that never really ends.

This is an inspiring idea in many ways, but from what I have seen; American and British business was not very responsive to it when lean ideas began to proliferate in the 1980's and 1990's. Gradual incremental improvement just sounded too slow. They needed things to get better now, not wait around for thousands of tiny fixes to gradually accumulate in the system.

So American and British organizations popularized the idea of the "kaizen blitz," a short period of highly-focused lean transformation where you did drop everything else and radically transform your business to a leaner, better form. In theory, this blitz would take many of those tiny little improvements and jam them into one frenzied weekend or week or month or quarter, then blast off the operation into a different stratosphere when work resumed.

It is an exciting idea, but has some issues:

It takes time to reprogram people with traditional mass-production mindsets into leaner ways of thinking, and a brief blitz may not be long enough to accomplish this. People end up just going through the motions for a while and then sliding back into systems they understand better.

Kaizen blitzes have a marketing aspect to them, with a lot of lean experts offering to come transform your organization in just few days or weeks for a low-low consultation bill. Some of these experts may be able to do what they claim, but many others have a fly-by-night feel reminiscent of the cheesy "investment seminars" and "body detox weekends" run by charlatans in airport hotel conference rooms. Like anything else, it probably sounds too good to be true for a reason.

Lean production is a method for learning about your organization so that you can improve it. The results of that organizational leaning process may take considerably longer to develop than it takes to simply learn the basics of lean production. I am not saying that lean transformations cannot have immediate results; they can and often do. It's just important to distinguish the way you think about your process from the results of that thinking. After all, even Toyota is still learning new things about how to make cars.

That last point is key for me as I ponder why the 5S process bogged down in my kitchen. Figuring out how to keep a kitchen organized properly for cooking is an ongoing process, one that I simply can't blast through completely in one week. I definitely can't blast through it in a week when I get so little uninterrupted time to pursue it.

So I am going to scale back and see this as just the first pass in a series of ongoing 5S procedures. I don't have the unobstructed time I need to properly organize the cabinets and fridge and freezer right now, so I won't. I will keep working on the countertops, a manageable goal, and return to the rest of it on the next pass.

Chapter 13: Poka Yoke and Childproofing

A major concern in any household with toddlers is safety. The little tykes just get into everything, especially if it's dangerous or off-limits. As a result, making your home safe for children (despite their best efforts) could not be more important.

We have learned one simple lesson while childproofing our house:

Active safety measures are not enough. You must have passive safety measures as well.

The difference between active and passive measures is simple. Does the safety measure rely on your constant attention and participation to be effective? If so, it's active. If not, it's passive.

The reason why this distinction is important: It's not enough to just "try really hard to keep an eye on the kids." Sooner or later, you will be distracted or careless, just for a moment, and when that happens, all bets are off. To keep your kids safe, you have no choice but to have a backup method that doesn't rely on your active attention.

For instance, until your kids are old enough to handle stairs without supervision, you really need to have baby gates. Your careful attention will eventually fail, if just for a second, and that is more than enough time for a nasty tumble to take place. The metal of the safety gate, on the other hand, is passively solid and unyielding every moment of every day whether you are paying attention or not.

The idea that active safety measures must be backed up by more passive measures is common outside of child care as well. Most people acknowledge that even if you drive very carefully, wearing seatbelts and having a car with airbags are still pretty good ideas. And every carpenter knows that whatever your experience level, protective goggles are a great investment.

In lean production, these passive safety or defect-prevention methods are referred to by the term "poka-yoke." Some observers translate poka-yoke as "idiot-proofing," which seems unnecessarily pejorative. I prefer the alternate translation, "mistake-proofing." Poka-yoke wants to make it impossible for people to make mistakes, whether through inattention, poor training, fatigue, or any other reason.

Industrial examples of poka-yoke are generally simple yet surprisingly effective physical "hacks." Taping a piece of cardboard over a machine input can make it impossible to put a piece of raw material in the wrong way. Installing a "dead man's switch" on a device can make it impossible for the operator to stick a vulnerable hand into a dangerous spinning mechanism while the machine is running (because the opening and the switch keeping the machine on are too far apart for the operator to simultaneously reach both). Using a simple torque-limiter on a screwdriver can make it impossible to over tighten screws. And so on. When a mistake becomes impossible, poka-yoke is happening.

Baby gates, outlet covers, doorknob spinners and cabinet locks are all poka-yoke measures that eliminate the kinds of household mistakes that can hurt a child. I am going to start looking around my home for more ways to reduce mistakes by making them otherwise impossible to perform. Here is a few I just thought up:

- Make all of your outside door locks deadbolts that require a key to engage the lock. If you have to have a key on you to lock the door, it is impossible to lock yourself out just because you left your keys inside.
- Block your door with your briefcase to make sure you won't forget it in the morning. It's impossible to overlook something you have to move to get out of the house.
- Take advantage of a built-in poka-yoke system and make sure your house outlets are polarized, making it impossible to put in a polarized plug the wrong way.

Chapter 14: The 2 Types of Muda

Muda is a Japanese word meaning futility; uselessness; idleness; superfluity; waste; wastage; wastefulness. There are 2 types of Muda.
1. Steps that create no value but are presently unavoidable due to the constraints of the current setup.
2. Steps that create no value and are avoidable in the current setup.

Obviously it's much harder to eliminate Type 1 muda than Type 2 muda, since the former require a total restructuring of your process. In practice, this means that as you pick off the low-hanging fruit of Type 2 wastes, you must tolerate Type 1 wastes until you have the resources to make more radical changes (and you must make them eventually if you want to have a truly lean operation).

An everyday-life example of a currently-unavoidable Type 1 waste is the large amount of waiting we have to tolerate right now. On days when only one parent is home with our toddlers (and often when both of us are home with them), there is very little time to work on anything besides direct and indirect childcare. Other tasks requiring any kind of concentration are limited to a rushed hour or two during the daily nap, plus a few extra hours some days when our babysitter is here, and whatever we have energy for between the toddlers' bedtime and ours.

We try to fit in what we can, but inevitably we can't get to everything we want to with so little time available. So, many tasks simply have to wait. This takes two general forms.

Some tasks are never started. Any task requiring a big block of time that cannot be paused midway are rarely attempted. We just don't have many of those time blocks, and those we do have are often spent catching up.

Most other tasks are broken into little pieces that can be done here and there over the course of a day or over several days.

An ideal lean process has of an unobstructed flow of value-creating steps from the moment a need is identified (by a customer, for instance) through to the moment that need is satisfied (by a product or outcome). That flow has no waiting, no buffers, no work-in-progress sitting around, just a smooth and ceaseless chain of value-creating activities from start to finish.

So, clearly many or most of our everyday processes aren't truly lean right now because they don't have this kind of flow at all. Indeed, they won't really have it until the toddlers become much more self-sufficient. How do we respond to this?

I am trying hard to avoid just throwing up my hands and giving up for the time being on our attempts at a leaner life. My understanding of lean techniques suggests that as we change to a leaner way of doing things, resources will become available that we never had before (such as time to work on other things). In other words, lean techniques don't have to be a casualty of our situation; they may actually be a remedy for our situation.

But it will take patience. Right now, we have a lot more time for picking off those minor Type-2 mudas than we have for more fundamental Type-1 muda elimination, and we will have to be satisfied with that. Meanwhile, I will hang on to the reasonable expectation that as Type-2 mudas are extinguished, we will find ourselves with more time to work towards the potentially greater rewards that come from quashing Type-1 problems.

Chapter 15: Seven Kinds of Waste

To review, the seven wastes (often called the "7 W's" or "seven muda," the Japanese word for waste) that are found in a production process are:
- Defects
- Inventory
- Motion
- Overprocessing
- Overproduction
- Transportation
- Waiting

Looking at the 7W's all together; you can see some patterns among them.

Most of them involve doing or having too much of something, whether it's keeping too much stuff on hand, moving people or objects around too much, or spending too much time doing things that aren't needed, making things that aren't needed, or even doing nothing at all.

Each kind of waste is intertwined with every other kind, to the point that any increase in one kind of waste often leads to an increase in other kinds of waste, and decreases in one kind of waste can lead to a decrease other kinds of waste.

Each kind of waste is both a practical problem and a camouflage for unresolved conceptual problems. Inventory buffers hide poor supply mechanisms; overprocessing hides defective work techniques; waiting hides faulty transportation patterns, and so on. Getting rid of each type of waste doesn't just solve the immediate problem; it uncovers the design issues that are being obscured by it.

Each kind of waste is an obstacle to flow. The highest goal of any lean process is for it to flow smoothly like a river from beginning to end. Friction wastes energy and resources, and leads to defective and unsatisfying results.

In these commonalities, a vision of lean production can start to take shape. A lean process is one which flows smoothly from start to finish with no obstacles or barriers. Anything that might block or slow the flow is eliminated, an effort that rapidly accelerates as reducing one form of waste in turn reduces other forms of related waste and a feedback loop develops. Fundamental conceptual problems that were obscured by waste are resolved and replaced by new, better visions. All of this keeps on happening, day in and day out, as the continuous process of improvement endlessly refines the process to achieve cheaper, easier, higher-quality results.

There is nothing magical about the number seven. The TPS (Toyota Production System) could easily have defined five forms of waste, or ten, or dozens. Many wasteful actions in the real world may actually fit into none of the classic categories, or into several. The 7W's are just rules of thumb to help identify the wasteful parts of a production process and start to correct them.

When thinking about creating a leaner everyday life, it's worth remembering that finding the seven wastes is the beginning of the process, not the end. It is not about how many waste categories you can check off, it is about whether the process is flowing more smoothly, more error-free, more cheaply, and more satisfactorily than it was before. Anything that gets in the way of those goals, whether it's clearly described by one of the 7W's or not, is a candidate for reduction or elimination.

In the next seven chapters we will look at each of the seven form of waste and where it can be found in everyday life.

Chapter 16: Defects

The Toyota Production System (TPS) describes seven different categories of waste (or muda) in the production process. The elimination of these wastes is the most important step in creating a lean production process. (Lean equal No Waste).

The seven muda are Defects, Inventory, Motion, Overprocessing, Overproduction, Transportation and Waiting. This time we'll talk about Defects.

There are a number of ways that defective elements can come into a production process.

Materials: Sometimes the raw materials used in a process are contaminated or of too low a quality and using these materials leads to some of the products being defective. (Getting bad parts from vendors is an example of this as well.)

Tools: Tools that are poor quality, poorly understood, poorly maintained, or not suited to a task can create defective products.

Training: When people do not understand a step in a process (or the process as a whole), they can easily make mistakes in their performance that will cause some of the products to be defective.

Design: Products that are poorly designed can include pieces that fit together incorrectly, movements that do not work smoothly, etc.

Pacing: When demand is not level, production can start to move too quickly (rushing), which leads to mistakes and thus defects. Demand being too low can cause similar problems as the pace begins to drag.

Defects are a major production problem because there are only three ways of dealing with them, all bad.

Overlook them: Go ahead and bolt that flawed windshield on the car and hope for the best. This can work for a while, but inevitably leads to a decline in the reputation and desirability of the product or outcome you are producing. Many argue that this approach is one of the things that led American and British car companies to decline at the end of the 20th century.

Reject them: Tossing out the flawed windshield rather than bolting it into a car protects your reputation, but it has a huge cost. The materials, labour, training, etc., that went into producing the windshield are lost. Too much of this, and your profitability goes out of the window. Piles of rejected parts also add to inventory issues.

Rework them: Putting the flawed windshield on a pile until some guys with tongs and glue can come around and bang it back into shape saves some of the investment you have in it, and the reworked product may be reliable enough to save your reputation. But it also has costs, eating up precious time, labour, storage space, tool use, and other resources that wouldn't have been necessary if the product had been defect-free to begin with.

In the old-style automobile companies before lean production came along, defects were seen as acceptable and unavoidable.

Cars would come down the line with parts bolted on incorrectly, glue that wouldn't hold, paint that wouldn't dry smooth, and a myriad of other problems. Instead of stopping the process to find out why each of these defects was happening (a big no-no); the defects would either be ignored or put aside for reworking. Entire lots behind car factories were filled with completed vehicles needing substantial fixes before they could be shipped out.

Lean automobile factories treat defects as a much more serious issue than did traditional factories. Workers are given permission to stop the production line any time a defect appears and use a problem-solving technique, such as the Five Whys, to locate the root cause of problems at their source. The assumption is that defects are not random occurrences, but are symptoms of systematic problems that will simply recur if not dealt with.

The reduction of defects is a difficult task, but it has many rewards. Fewer defects means less wasted materials, less inventory space for defective products, lower labour costs for rework, higher reliability and customer satisfaction, and higher worker satisfaction due to the increased personal responsibility.

Reducing defects is so important to lean production that a whole variant system, Six-Sigma, was created at Motorola to deal with defects. (More on Six-Sigma in my other books; **1. Lean Six Sigma (Cost Reduction Strategies) 2. Design for Six Sigma (DFSS)**.) However, defects are just one source of waste in production, and reduced defects are just one of the positive results of a continuously-improving lean process.

Bringing lean concepts back into everyday life, it is often not hard to see where defects begin to crop up in day to day processes. Burnt toast leads to waste as we either have to choke down the char (ignore it), throw away the piece entirely (reject it), or scrape off the char with a knife (rework it). Failing to figure out why the dryer is staining clothes leads to some shirts being relegated to rag duty or being worn under sweaters. Using bad running shape leads to calf and shin injuries.

And in our case, the dishwasher that doesn't get dishes properly clean leads to waste as some dishes end up being rewashed, sometimes multiple times. The lean approach to this issue is to stop using the dishwasher entirely, trace the problem back to its root cause, and deal with it before moving on and creating more defects. Unfortunately, two visits from the repairman haven't divulged the root cause, so the defects, and waste, continue. It's a target for continuous improvement efforts in the future.

Defects can be found as an input, a transitional state, or an output of production processes, and must be stamped out at each point for the process to be truly lean.

Chapter 17: Inventory

From the lean perspective, inventory is not an asset, it is a liability. This is a reversal of the positive way some see excess inventory, as a "stockpile," a "cache," or a "surplus". Inventory is a liability because no pile of stuff is truly free of cost. To keep an inventory you have to:
- **Put it somewhere:** Pay for and maintain a space for it.
- **Keep it in decent condition and well-organized:** Set aside resources for maintenance and organization.
- **Find uses for it to justify accumulating it to begin with:** Hold yourself back at times when you should be making changes and going other directions instead.

The highest cost of inventory is that it can hide a multitude of procedural sins that really need to be dealt with.

In the traditional car factories that lean production later transformed, massive amounts of space were set aside for extra parts, extra tools, and extra cars that had been produced but were not ready to be shipped. These inventories cost a great deal of money to house and maintain costs that had to be either absorbed by the company or passed on to the buyer. Both of these are bad for the car company.

Although it was nice to have a few extra parts or completed units sitting around "just in case," having large inventories of these things also kept managers from noticing important problems. With a large inventory of extra parts at hand, a worker trying to bolt a defective part onto a car can simply toss it aside and grab one of the extras without having to wonder why the part was defective to begin with. When a large number of completed cars are sitting in a lot behind the factory, it's unnecessary to iron out chronic procedural issues that cause delays or even complete stops in the production line from time to time.

Lean production methods do allow for some small inventories in a process (enough to cover the time needed to bring new supplies to the line, for instance), but large inventories are totally eliminated. This is frightening because it removes a number of traditional safety nets, but it is powerful and effective for that same reason. After a period of adjustment, small inventories make the process more sensitive to its underlying problems and more dependent upon people resolving them quickly and completely. In addition, the organization gets back all of the space, money, labour, and time it was spending maintaining those large inventories and can use them for things that more directly benefit the customer.

Large inventories can have the same negative consequences in everyday life that they have in the business world. For instance, I recently thinned-out our collection of knives in our kitchen knife drawer. I found to my surprise that many of the blades were dull, some were missing pieces, and some were not being maintained properly because we could always grab another older, lesser knife that would work "good enough for now." Now that we have only a few knives we truly like using, we can find them more quickly, maintain them more easily, and have freed up space in the drawer for other things.

Chapter 18: Motion

In the lean perspective, the muda of motion or movement refers to unnecessary movement of people as they perform tasks that are necessary to complete the product or process. Motion is deemed unnecessary when it adds no value to the product being produced or process being completed.

Traditional auto assembly plants tended to have a great deal of wasted movement as specific personnel assigned to various tasks (housekeeping, tool repair, parts supply, quality inspection, and sick-day filling-in) bustled around the plant trying to keep things running smoothly. The classic book on lean automobile production, The Machine That Changed the World, described the aisles at traditional car factories as being full of personnel running from place to place, none of them directly contributing anything of value to the cars being made.

Lean automobile factories, on the other hand, are noticeable for the lack of personnel found in the narrow aisles. The tasks of housekeeping, tool repair, parts inspection, quality inspection and filling in for sick workers are all performed by the assembly teams themselves without leaving their own work area. This is possible because the assembly teams, being the ones actually assembling the cars, are the best authorities on what is necessary to keep their work proceeding smoothly.

There are many ways to find examples of unnecessary motion in everyday life. These wastes fall into two main types.

1. Unnecessary movement of the person through space, i.e., pointless walking around. A good example of this is making unneeded trips back and forth to the garbage can next to the garage because trash day keeps catching you off-guard and wastebaskets fill up at erratically different rates.

2. Unnecessary movement of the person's limbs and other body parts, i.e., waving your hands around more than necessary. A good everyday example of this is stopping every few seconds to open a trash pail to toss out trimmings while you cook a meal.

There are a number of ways to handle each of these issues. For instance, establishing a set trash routine and correctly calibrating the size of wastebaskets to match the demand for them can help reduce all those trips to the dumpster. And keeping a "junk bowl" on the counter to fill with various trimmings as you cook, to be dumped in the trash all at once when you are done, can cut down (pun unintended but inevitable) on those repeated trashcan openings.

There is a big counterargument to be made when the Motion issue is brought up in everyday life rather than in a factory: Human bodies require plenty of motion, and modern lifestyles really could often use a little more of it for health reasons rather than a little less.

This is true as far as it goes, with some caveats. First, not all motion is good for you. Repetitive strain injuries, most common with the second type of motion listed above, can cause horrible discomfort and any wasted movements causing are well worth eliminating for health reasons.

Second, it really all comes down to the value question. If the motion you are achieving (e.g., trips to the garbage can next to the garage) gives little of value to you or the people you care about, what is the point of continuing this wasteful practice just to get a little movement into your life? Better to spend some of your time doing a movement you enjoy (swimming, walking, cycling, etc.) to burn those calories and build your cardiovascular system, where the movement gives both health benefits and something of value to your day.

Motion may not be the biggest form of waste in a process, but it can be the most aggravating, as anyone who has had to make one too many trips to the grocery store because she forgot one item can tell you. It is well worth pondering when you are trying to make your everyday life leaner.

Nothing messes up a house, in my eye, like dirty clothes and messy dishes. Worse, you can't just shove them in a closet and forget about them the way you can with wayward books. You can't put them away unless you process them.

They are recurring. No matter what you do today, there will be more dirty clothes and dishes tomorrow. Since you can't escape from these processes for any significant period of time, there is good reason to try to improve them by getting rid of waste and making them leaner.

They are low-hanging fruit. Although finances or diet or parenting are important issues, identifying and getting rid of waste in those areas is more difficult and less concrete than just figuring out how to keep the dishes washed.

For any or all of those reasons, laundry and dishes still haunt my everyday lean production efforts. For example, I noticed today that even when I do laundry every single day, sometimes a huge amount of clothes will appear at the bottom of the laundry chute in the morning. This is always discouraging, since it makes it very hard to level the demand for laundry, and I know it will take me days just to catch up on the backlog.

Why does it keep happening? Partly it has to do with living with toddlers. Toddlers require somewhat more clothing changes than adults, and at more unpredictable intervals. Levelling their demand is hard.

But that is not all of it. Looking over the dirty clothes in the chute on mornings like this, I see adult clothes that were worn several days before, even though just I sorted the dirty clothes yesterday.

The problem is obvious. Somebody is stashing dirty clothes somewhere else instead and putting them down the chute in occasional batches! Why would anyone (or several anyones) do this when it is so easy to just immediately put the clothes down the chute as they are used?

My question is why do hospital employees always stashed extra supplies around the office, making it hard to really streamline operations? The simple answer was that people didn't trust the system to provide supplies when they needed them, so they stashed supplies as a "buffer" to get them by if something went wrong. The solution to the problem, then, was to build more trust with the system. People will feel comfortable running on the thinner margins called for by lean processes when they know the supplies will always show up when they need them.

I suppose trust is part of our problem, too. Over the holidays, especially, it was hard to get all of the laundry processed the way it was supposed to be. As a result, too many clothes got washed but not dried, dried but not folded, or folded but not put away. If people don't trust that their process will flow without obstacles from beginning to end, they feel the desire (or freedom) to build up stashes here and there rather than put everything directly into the system that isn't getting it done anyway.

The solution to our problem, then, is partly one of discipline. The system only works if it is worked as it should be, every single day. Wavering off the path for even a short time leads to delays, mistrust, non-level demand…in short, all of the problems that lean production tries to solve.

But the problem also suggests that there are still kinks in the system that we still need to work out. It's futile to try to overcome a bad system by just increasing your personal discipline therefore I would suggest that you fix the system, and then eliminate the hoarding. Until you build trust, you are just punishing people for trying to do the right thing for the patient. Hoarding is a workaround; eliminate the need for the workaround.

Chapter 19: Overprocessing

Overprocessing is simply the act of handling, working on, or otherwise dealing with something more than is necessary. Since processing anything, in any way, consumes resources like time, labour, and space, doing it any more processing than you absolutely have to is a waste.

Overprocessing can occur for many reasons.

Lack of obvious completion cues: If you have ever run a dishwasher full of clean dishes again because nobody told you it was "done," you've experienced this kind of overprocessing.

Lack of organization: When items are hard to locate, you are forced to sort through many items over and over again as you try to track down what you are looking for. You are overprocessing your stuff because it isn't organized well.

Lack of clear direction: Sometimes we handle things just to feel like we are doing something useful with them. Then we put them down with nothing having been accomplished, and come back to them later to put them around aimlessly again. This is one method of maintaining a "procrastination field" that seems like work, but is not.

Improper completion of tasks: When you do something wrong, you often have to do it all over again just to set things right. For instance, accidentally I often used to use adult laundry detergent to wash our baby clothes, which meant I had to wash them again to avoid irritating our newborns' sensitive skin. (I have since solved this problem with the simple habit of storing the baby detergent next to the baby clothes basket, so I never see one without seeing the other.)

In the traditional automobile industry, this need to rectify defects was the most common source of overprocessing-related waste. Fast-moving assembly lines and quota-focused supervisors didn't leave time for dealing with mistakes, so they were passed down the line until the end where a team of skilled rework technicians would spend time fixing all of the accumulated mistakes. All of that rework was overprocessing, work that could have been avoided had it been done right the first time.

As we go through these forms of waste, it is obvious that they tend to be related to each other. For instance, the more inventory you have to deal with, the more wasted motion you will experience as workers move around to deal with all the extra stuff. By the same token, the more defects you generate during production, the more overprocessing you will do as you waste time fixing things that never should have been broken to begin with. This interdependence can make solving problems rather knotty at times, but it also means that sometimes solving one issue will solve several other related issues at the same time, a nice bonus.)

There are many opportunities for overprocessing in everyday life. Handling the same piece of mail over and over again because you haven't responded to it or filed it away, washing the same dishes or clothes multiple times because they are never done properly, having the same conversation over and over again because you never get to the underlying issue.

Overprocessing is insidious because it often seems cheap and often seems unavoidable.

However, there are many ways to handle overprocessing in everyday processes.

- Instituting a "handle each piece of mail just once" policy for postal mail (or an "Inbox Zero" policy for email).
- Going through a Five-Whys procedure to figure out why clothes or dishes aren't getting done without defects.
- Doing some self-examination to uncover why you can't speak your mind instead of having the same conversation loop popping up repeatedly. And so on.

There are as many possible solutions are there are possible problems. The important thing to remember is that overprocessing is a problem. You can't avoid processing things in a production process: That is what a production process is. But processing things that do not need to be processed (or processing them more times than they need to be) doesn't help you create what you are trying to create, which means that it is an obstacle rather than an accomplishment.

Chapter 20: Overproduction

Overproduction is simply producing anything that doesn't need to be produced. There are two basic forms:

1. Producing something nobody wants.
2. Producing something that people do want, but including something in it that nobody wants.

Going back to the traditional car company, overproduction includes not only making cars for which there is no customer demand; it also includes making car features for which there is no demand, even in otherwise desirable car models.

Overproduction is the most important kind of waste; indeed, all other forms of waste can be viewed as a kind of subset of overproduction.

It's not hard to see why overproduction is the worst of the seven muda. There is nothing more wasteful than producing something customers don't want. No improvement in any of the other wastes (reducing defects, getting rid of excess motion, etc.) will have any effect if the entire process is itself a waste of time because it is trying to meet a demand that doesn't exist.

There are some historical roots for this concern about overproduction in Japanese car companies. Back when the Japanese auto industry was just getting going, it lacked the money and other resources needed to maintain massive production inventories until demand picked up. Overproduction simply wasn't an option. If a car was built, it had to be sold, and quickly. This meant that a system had to be developed to accurately sense current customer demand and immediately translate that demand into production as cheaply and effectively as possible. That system was lean production.

To stamp out wasteful overproduction, you need to pay attention to many things.

Continuously gathering accurate information about customer demand and quickly communicating that back to the production process.

Building strong long-term relationships with suppliers, workers and customers so that large shifts in customer demand can be met with flexible solutions rather than mindlessly and wastefully churning out surplus inventory or laying off employees.

Creatively finding ways to level demand while still allowing for wide variety and high responsiveness in production.

Engaging in strict editing to remove anything from the product or outcome that customers don't really want, even if their engineers or designers think customers should want them.

The ultimate goal is to create a process where the only thing produced, at any point, is something that creates value for the customer. Everything in a production process that fails to fit this definition is not just pointless, it is a hindrance.

In everyday life, it can be hard to find examples of overproduction without a little soul-searching. Most people feel like they barely have time to take care of the necessities, so the notion that they are generating anything unneeded seems laughable. In the busiest life, however, there are opportunities for editing.

For instance, in our household, it's ironic that we have a kitchen overflowing with food but never have anything to eat, closets overflowing with clothes but never have anything to wear, and a Receiver full of recorded TV shows but never anything to watch. Each of these situations screams of overproduction at some point.

We are buying and washing and keeping the wrong kinds of clothes, which wastes our time and effectively hides the right clothes from us by pushing them to the back of overfull closets.

We are buying too much food that we won't eat and ingredients we will never use.

We record TV shows based on our aspirations rather than our realities, leading to us filling up our receiver with things we wish we would watch (thoughtful, complex dramas and documentaries) rather than things we will watch at the end of a long day (sitcoms and other junk-tv).

In short, we aren't overproducing because we are doing too much: We are overproducing because we are doing too much of the wrong things. Our solution isn't to do less, it's to become more sensitive to our real lifestyle and our real demands and try to meet them as effectively as possible.

Even in everyday life, overproduction may be the grandest waste category of them all, so it's worth thinking about. You will never really reduce waste and get your everyday processes lean if you are making things nobody really wants.

Chapter 21: Transportation

This time we will talk about Transportation.

Transportation waste is generated whenever you move objects around unnecessarily. (This is related to the waste of motion, which is generated whenever you move people around unnecessarily.)

Obviously, if you are manufacturing something, some movement of objects is going to be necessary to get it produced. So how do you know when that movement of objects is necessary versus unnecessary? The acid test for whether something is useful movement versus transportation waste is the same question you can use to identify all other kinds of waste in your process.

Does doing this increase the value of our produced item (or outcome) for the customer?

If the answer is "No," you are talking about transportation waste rather than necessary movement of parts and supplies.

Hauling stuff around unnecessarily obviously consumes time, energy, labour, and money that could be used for something else. However, there are also some less obvious consequences of needlessly moving stuff around. For example:

Increasing inventories: When stuff gets moved around a lot for little reason, it inevitably piles up in various places, robbing space from more useful activities.

Increasing defects: Every time you move something around, you risk getting it dirty, damaging it, or losing track of it.

Increased waiting: Moving things around unnecessarily means they will often not be where they are needed, prompting a lot of waiting around for it to get to where it's supposed to be.

In the traditional auto industry before lean production, there was an enormous amount of time and energy spent moving parts and supplies here and there between factories and within factories. All of that movement was partly the result (and partly the cause) of the large inventories of surplus parts, supplies, and even completed vehicles sitting around the facilities. According to The Machine That Changed the World, as objects were shifted needlessly here and there throughout the production process, the aisles of automobile plants were constantly jammed full of frenzied workers struggling to get what they needed when they needed it.

The lean production process looks for this kind of unnecessary motion and eliminates it. In the lean automobile plant, parts are delivered by suppliers to workers on the line immediately after they are produced and exactly when the workers need them. This eliminates all of the pointless shuffling of parts from loading docks to warehouses to secondary storage and finally to the production line itself.

Of course, this sort of delicately coordinated movement is only possible because lean producers also try to reduce transportation waste at a much larger scale by locating their facilities (and those of their vendors) geographically close to one another. Indeed, all of these operations are also located as close as possible to the customers they will serve, reducing another kind of transportation waste generated when products are shipped to customers. (The reduction of wasted movement is one big reason why so many Japanese automobile producers have factories in the United States and Europe. Nothing adds to a car's sticker price like a long ocean voyage.)

In everyday life, there are many opportunities to reduce the amount of time and energy we spend hauling things around unnecessarily.

An example gets into those larger-scale transportation questions that led lean manufacturers to change where they located their factories.

Many suburbanites turn grocery shopping into a multi-stage food transportation process. Food is bought in massive batches at the store and then brought home, where it is put into a freezer. From the freezer, the food eventually moves to the fridge when it's time to thaw it for dinner. Then, days or weeks or even months later, the food is finally cooked and eaten. This doesn't even count all of the movement of food around as you re-organize the fridge or freezer after buying even more food.

There is another way to handle all of this with less wasted motion: Buy only the food you need for at most a day or two of meals, and then bring it directly back to the kitchen where it will immediately be cooked and eaten. No need for large freezers or stuffed cabinets, no need for jostling stuff around in your pantry. Food shows up only when it is needed, is only transported once from the store to the kitchen, and doesn't stick around.

Is it possible to actually live this way? In the suburbs, maybe not. If you live in a city where a grocery store may well be a hundred yards from your front door, it may be possible to live like this. (I've often heard that this is the way people live in urban European cities, where there's little market for the huge refrigerators and freezers and pantries Americans are used to.) Whether this particular example is realistic for you or not, it shows the issues that come up when you start thinking about reducing transportation waste. The very basic assumptions of your system (i.e., where you choose to live) have a direct influence on the wastes your everyday processes will have to deal with.

As you try to reduce the waste in your everyday processes, think about the ways you might be moving things around unnecessarily. Yes, you will always need to move some things around to get your work done (those dishes won't put themselves away), so the key is to focus on the truly unneeded movement of things.

How do you know what movement isn't needed? Ask the everyday-life version of the question I mentioned earlier: "Does this movement of stuff add real value to the everyday lives of the people I care about (including me)?" If not, it's transportation waste, and it's time to ditch it and find another way of doing things.

One warning: A common way to try to reduce transportation waste is to increase the size of your batches. For example, taking more items with you in your arms whenever you go downstairs, saving yourself some downstairs trips.

Try not to do this! Lean production principles argue that larger batch sizes tend to cause more problems than they solve. Instead of relying entirely on making fewer trips and carrying larger payloads, look more deeply at the process itself: Why are you carrying all of this stuff around anyway? Is it all necessary? Would some of it be better located close at hand rather than down in the basement? Reducing transportation waste is ultimately about getting rid of wasted movements, not just increasing their capacity.

Chapter 22: Waiting

A big component of the Toyota Production System (TPS) is its identification of the categories of waste (or muda) in the typical production process. Getting rid of these seven wastes is the main goal of a lean production process. (Lean Equal No Waste.)

Waiting is probably the easiest form of waste to understand. Whenever people, equipment or processes are idle when they could instead be creating value for a customer, you are generating waiting-related waste.

In the traditional automobile factory, the production process often finds itself waiting for.

Supplies: If supplies are not available in time to put them into a car, the process halts until they are available. (I saw this happened first-hand on a tour of a BMW mini plant, which ground to a halt in front of our eyes when a snowstorm on the UK stopped the flow of parts into the factory.)

Equipment: If equipment has not been configured for the next task, the process halts until it has been reconfigured. This can take a great deal of time on the huge single-purpose machinery of traditional factories; Henry Ford's automobile plants shut down for months when they had to be reconfigured for a new model.

Completion of preceding steps: If the preceding step in a process is not completed in time, the subsequent step will be idle until it has caught up. Traditional factories use push-style systems that rely on guesswork and predictions to judge when steps need to be completed, and these forecasts often go wrong in the real-life chaos of the plant.

Quality Inspection: When a production process produces a high number of defects, the product will be forced to wait for time-consuming quality inspection at various points in the process (especially at the end) to ensure that a defective product does not go out to customers.

Rework: Similarly, when many defects find their way into a product during the production process, various parts or even the entire product must wait for extensive repair and rework to remove these defects before the product can be shipped.

Customer Demand: If the customers do not want what the factory is producing, the factory will eventually be forced to go idle and furlough its workforce until demand picks up or the factory is retooled for a new product line.

Although it is often worthwhile to pause in a production process (to solve a problem, for instance), none of the above examples of waiting adds any value to the product for the consumer. On the other hand, all of the above examples of waiting add to the costs and headaches of the manufacturer. This is why waiting is generally seen as a waste by the lean perspective, and why its reduction or elimination is seen as an unequivocal gain for the production process.

Lean production techniques include a number of solutions for the problem of waiting.
- Pull-style coordination systems are used to make sure that supply deliveries and manufacturing steps are

completed "just in time" for the subsequent process requiring them, and not a moment after (or before).
- Quick-change equipment procedures are used, such as the famous single-minute exchange of dies (SMED) that drastically reduced the time it took to reconfigure an automobile body panel press for its next task.
- An intolerance of defects becomes standard procedure. Any defects are quickly traced back to their source using a diagnostic technique such as the "Five Why's," and prevented in the future rather than being dumped downstream into subsequent processes. A lean process strives for such a low defect rate that almost no quality inspection or rework is necessary before products are shipped out to customers.
- Small batches of work are done and flexible multi-purpose machinery are used, allowing the whole process to be rapidly reshaped to match quickly-changing customer appetites. As a result, the workflow is stable, the process is responsive to its constituents, and mistaken predictions of future demand are unable to sideline the operation.

Although reducing waiting has many advantages, it is not easy. Running on the thin time margins found in lean production requires a great deal of trust in the process. Moreover, in the early stages of a lean transformation, waiting is often increased as the process stops continuously to deal with systemic problems. However, as the kinks get worked out, the opposite generally becomes true; lean production processes then become much less prone to interruption than more traditional processes and waiting becomes a negligible issue.

Taking this out of the factory and into everyday life, it isn't hard to find examples where poorly-organized processes suffer from unnecessary waiting. Postponing necessary maintenance on household equipment can lead to long waits for repairs to be made to the car or lawnmower. Tolerating careless work in the kitchen leads the need to check and recheck food before it hits the table to make sure an important ingredient hasn't been left out, pushing dinner later. Failing to run the dishwasher or laundry "until you get a full load" can lead to long waits for clean mugs or dress pants. And so on.

When considering the ways that waiting impacts everyday life processes and how it can be eliminated, it's worth remembering that different forms of waste are usually connected. You cannot get rid of waiting while you still tolerate a lot of defects, because defects lead to waiting. Excess motion or transportation also lead to waiting, as do all of the other forms of waste in some way or another.

Chapter 23: Kanban and Fine Tuning

One key difference between lean production and traditional mass-production is how necessary supplies are provided. Traditional mass production systems tend to use a push system in which the amount of supplies, and the schedule for generating them, is determined by guesswork rather than actual demand. The producer orders a certain amount of supplies, an act that requires a lot of estimation and capital outlay ahead of time.

The supplies show up at the factory on a predetermined date, where they must be stored until they will be used. If the earlier guess was wrong, there will either be too many supplies (if demand is lower than expected) or too few (if demand is higher than expected). In terms of waste, any errors in guessing how many supplies should be pushed to the factory by the contractual agreement will result in either extra inventory or extra waiting, both of which are costly.

Lean production methods take a different approach to supply, choosing to pull the supplies from the supplier (either internal or external) according to the demand for them right now rather than making guesses about the future. This is often handled simply using a "supermarket" style system called kanban.

In a kanban-style system, when a process nears the end of its supplies, a signal is generated that tells the supplier that more of the supply should be made. The supplier makes more supplies and delivers them back to the production line where they are immediately put to use. There are no extra inventories and no long periods of waiting for supplies, since they are generated as needed and only as needed.

The kanban approach is much more responsive to customer demand and much more efficient for everyone involved. However, a kanban system requires a great deal of trust between a supplier and a producer. Both must work hard to keep demand as level as possible to avoid overwhelming each other with too-intense demand or too many unneeded surpluses. Both must also feel secure in their long-term relationship, since they will be responding to customer demand together rather than guaranteeing profits by enforcing pre-set supply volumes regardless of circumstances.

A critical component of the kanban system is the kanban card, the specific signal that is sent to the supplier to indicate more supplies are needed. The signal can be as simple as the empty supply container being sent back to the upstream supplier, or it can be an actual card with specific information about the part that is needed and in what amount. It can even be part of an electronic kanban system where the necessary information is sent electronically rather than physically, saving further by eliminating some wasted object transportation and personnel motion.

Whichever form it takes, the kanban "card" is the signal that says what kind and how much work must be done by the supplier or process immediately upstream, and it must be calibrated carefully to match actual demand.

A simple kanban signal I use in everyday life is the laundry basket. Our laundry gets sorted into four separate baskets. When one of the baskets is full at laundry time, that basket of clothes gets washed.

In this scheme, choosing a proper-sized laundry basket is important. If a basket is too large, it will take too long to fill with laundry and the clothes it holds won't get washed often enough. If the basket is too small, it will fill too quickly and the clothes will get washed more often than they are really required. In other words, with wrong-sized baskets acting as our kanban signals, our production of clean clothes won't match our demand for them.

To get things calibrated more precisely, I recently switched the small basket for children's' clothes, which was filling too quickly and leaving us with more clean kids' clothes than we needed, with the large basket for white clothes, which was filling too slowly and leaving us with too few clean white shirts and socks. The idea is to level out the demand so that each basket will fill in a similar amount of time, allowing me to stick to a "one load a day" washing schedule that allows our clothes to be washed at a pace that is neither too fast nor too slow to meet our demand. Switching the smaller basket to the whites and the larger basket to kids' clothes recalibrated the system and solved the problem.

(For another example of everyday kanban, here is a good approach to keeping paper towels and bath tissue supplied steadily at home, one that I have started using myself.)

Switching to a pull-based system rather than a push-based system can have a big impact on the efficiency of the overall system, but like everything in the lean approach, there are always more fine-tuning and constant small improvements to be made.

Chapter 24: Little Guy Versus the Big Boss

To successfully make a transition to lean production, you must have the support of top people in the organization. There are simply too many fundamental, revolutionary changes that have to happen when you become lean to try to get it all done as some kind of "rogue operation." You will need to re-examine your relationships with your workers, your management, your suppliers, your customers, and every single task you perform. And you will have to do it continuously, over and over again, forever. It will never happen for real if the Big Boss isn't on board.

However, it's equally true that real change will never happen if the Little Guy isn't on board. Lean production methods push responsibility and control down the organizational hierarchy to the people directly adding value for the customer. Workers and managers at all levels are just different kinds of problem solvers, and all are expected to be continuously be thinking about ways to improve the lean production process to get rid of waste and become more responsive.

As my knowledge of lean techniques grows and my enthusiasm for making our everyday lives leaner builds, I have been increasingly taking the role of Big Boss on these little lifestyle initiatives in our home. That is a good thing in many ways; it's important to have an influential leader giving support to any lean transformation attempt.

However, I have been making the mistake of overlooking the crucial role of the Little Guy. I have been spending too much time trying to nudge, wheedle, cajole, and nag my spouse into obeying and supporting the lean everyday processes I am coming up with, with little success. I have made many attempts to explain why these methods are better, but that doesn't seem to be enough to guarantee the cooperation and enthusiasm I am looking for.

Since my wife and I spend a great deal of time apart on weekdays, I can overlook these implementation issues by simply ignoring them and living a separate existence when she is not around. But that is wasteful, since it guarantees a lot of repair work to get "the system" back into its accustomed shape when the weekend ends and I am in total control again.

It also misses the point. My spouse is an equal participant in our everyday lives. Even though I am the unquestioned authority on lean methods, I am not the only person who washes dishes or makes meals or does laundry or any of a thousand other things necessary to get through a week in our lives. Ignoring my spouse's actions or trying to paper-over them with frenzied activity when she is not around (as though I'm having an affair with lean production methods!) just isn't the right approach.

Instead, I should be doing what lean production says I should do. Pushing responsibility down the organisational chart and pushing communication up the organisational chart. I should be involving my wife in the transformation, getting her thoughts on where the processes work and where they need improvement.

Getting her input will help her feel more committed to the improvement project, but it goes beyond such self-serving outcomes. She is a front-line worker in our everyday lives, so she has to have a lot of ideas about how we could do things better. Even worse, as an ongoing participant in these processes, she will doubtlessly have more ideas as we go along, especially if she is truly engaged with the continuous improvement project. Ignoring all of these ideas (and potential ideas) is foolhardy and might even be more counterproductive than the resentment she is bound to feel at having a bunch of new processes forced upon her with no room for discussion.

Changing to a lean organization model really involves a fundamental change in how you see the participants. I am not the guru concocting grand schemes for my wife the line-worker to implement. We are partners, each of us doing crucial problem-solving to make the processes continuously better in large ways and small. It won't work unless everyone is on board, whether Big Boss or Little guy.

That is hard to accept. I am not sure how exactly to get my wife involved in this project the way she needs to be for it to work, and many business leaders don't know how to get their workers truly involved in their lean projects either. It is easier just to lay down a set of process improvements developed at the highest levels and let the workers just do it whether they like it or not, but that isn't a recipe for long term success.

I will be thinking a great deal more about how to get everyone involved in the continuous improvement of our everyday processes using lean production methods. After all, these issues with ownership and consensus and buy-in will only become more pronounced when the kids are no longer toddlers and they, too, become part of our getting our everyday life processes done.

Chapter 25: Toward a Lean Laundry

Laundry is one of the most mundane tasks that people deal with in everyday life, but it is also one of the most rewarding. Who doesn't get a pleasant feeling from looking at a closet or drawer full of clean, folded clothes? There is so much potential there.

Unfortunately, it is easy for laundry processes to get messed up. Things can get so bad that you never seem to get that pleasant feeling anymore because you never are done with your laundry, even for a single day.

I have been there. In our household, the laundry system went like this:
- Pile up dirty clothes in various places around the bedrooms. Baskets are nice, but are often filled to the point that you can't see them anymore below the piles.
- When the piles get too annoying, dump them down to the laundry room.
- Soon the bin in the laundry room becomes overfilled and its door pops open, spilling dirty clothes onto the floor.
- Take the piles of dirty clothes in the laundry room bin and on the floor and sort them into still more piles (on the floor) by colour, fabric, etc.
- Wash a load and try to remember to transfer it over to the dryer within a day or so, before it gets mildew-smelling.
- If you forget to transfer them over, run the wet clothes through the washer again to get rid of the mouldy smell. Then run them through the dryer.

- Get the clean clothes out of the dryer within another day or so and put them in a basket.
- Take the basket upstairs and leave it around when something else inevitably distracts you.
- Eventually fold the clothes in the basket that is been sitting on a long seat for two days and try to remember to put the clothes away.
- Eventually put the clothes away and leave the empty basket lying around a bedroom.
- Return to step 1.

Yes, it was not a great system. We were constantly running out of clean clothes that were folded, put away and ready to go. We never had any idea of whether certain clothes were clean or dirty and where to find them. And we had a very messy house (nothing looks as messy as laundry, in my opinion).

The solution to our laundry issues was to make the laundry process more like a Japanese car factory, i.e., a lean production process. To make the process leaner, the first step was to identify the muda, or waste, in the process. Let's quickly run through the seven wastes (muda) identified in lean production and see how our laundry system measured up.

1. **Defects:** Defective laundry was unfortunately visible and common in our system. Forget taking care of stains or anything unusual. We were struggling to simply get the laundry clean and put away. We did sometimes even get stuck wearing dirty clothes again because there was nothing appropriate clean, a great example of people just ignoring defects rather than dealing with them.

2. **Inventory:** We had piles of clothes (clean, dirty, or somewhere in between) lying all over the house. This made for a messy home with a lot of wasted space, and good luck finding your nice pants before you need to leave for work!

3. **Movement:** We spent a lot of time traipsing up and down stairs trying to find clothes and laundry baskets. In the US the laundry chute saved virtually no effort at all, as any load would end up involving multiple trips up and down the stairs anyway and in the UK we have no laundry chute.

4. **Overproduction:** We seldom generated clean clothes faster than we needed them. The opposite was almost always true. However, our production was extremely un-level, with us usually being way behind in laundry or, after a massive days-long binge to catch up, having far more clothes than we needed right away.

5. **Overprocessing:** Failing to change clothes over from the washer to the dryer promptly meant that we were washing many loads twice to get rid of the mouldy smell. Failing to get clothes out of the dryer promptly left us with a lot of very-wrinkled clothes that needed to be ironed or run through the "fluff" cycle again. For all of our failure to do enough laundry, we were washing some clothes a lot more than they needed to be.

6. **Transportation:** We moved clothes around a lot as they went from dirty to clean to dry to folded to put away. We did the same thing with laundry baskets, moving them

from place to place as we processed clothes. This often led to the baskets being misplaced for their next use: We did need an empty basket in the laundry room to put a load of clean clothes in, say, and it'd be up in a bedroom on the first floor.

7. **Waiting:** Piles of clothes in various states spent a lot of time sitting around various spots in our house waiting to be dealt with. We often had more clothes to wear, but they weren't always the right clothes. The right clothes were too often in a washer or dryer or pile somewhere, rather than in our closet.

It is obvious that there was a lot of waste in our laundry process, which is why I am talking about it in such detail. The more waste there is in a process, the greater the potential for improvement by adopting lean methods.

I will explain how we "leaned" our laundry in the next chapter. For now, to start lean-ifying a process that you are unhappy with, a good first step is to think it through using the checklist of wastes (muda) above. When you focus on the right problems, obvious solutions start to present themselves.

Chapter 26: Lean-ifying Laundry at Home

In the last chapter, I explained that we are using lean production principles to improve our personal laundry procedures because our old way of doing laundry was full of wasted time, effort, money, motion and defects.

After noting where the seven wastes of lean production showed up in our laundry process, we started our improvement efforts. Here is how our new lean laundry process works:

Getting dirty clothes in: All laundry (adults, kids, casual, formal, whatever) goes down to the laundry room. No exceptions. Clothes requiring special attention (stain remover, etc.) are tied in a loose knot to indicate this.

Sorting: Every single day, I sort the clothes in the bin at the laundry room into one of four laundry baskets next to the washer (colours, whites, toddler clothes, and reds). It takes just a minute or two.

Washing: As soon as the daily sorting is done (it takes just a minute or two), I look over the baskets. If any of the baskets is full, the clothes in that basket are loaded into the washer and it is run. If multiple baskets are full, I load whichever basket seems fullest at the time. If none are full, no laundry today!

Drying: After I put a load into the washer, I move a magnet to indicate this on a simple chart I drew on our kitchen whiteboard.

At lunchtime, I check the chart and if the magnet for "Washer" is on "Full," I move the wet clothes over to the dryer and run it. (I update this chart as I finish tasks to keep me from forgetting where things are in the process.)

Folding: In the late afternoon or after dinner, I pull one piece of clothes at a time from the dryer and fold it at the folding table nearby.

Putting away: As the clean clothes are folded, they go into a collapsible mesh laundry basket. I carry this basket upstairs, put the clothes away, and fold the basket up into its tiny flat storage shape. Then the basket goes back to the laundry room, where it will be waiting for the next morning's sorting.

I have been using this system for a few months now, and it has greatly improved the ease and success of our laundry. Let's see how it stacks up against the seven forms of waste I identified in our old laundry system.

1. **Defects:** Only doing one load a day, I am more able to get the laundry done completely and with fewer mistakes than when I was doing laundry infrequently.

2. **Inventory:** Instead of piles of clothes in various states (dirty, clean, and folded) all over the house, there are only three places for clothes to be. In the laundry room, in the washer or dryer, or in the closet. With baskets being put back to laundry room after clothes are put away, there are no more clothes baskets lying all over the house, either. All of this makes for a tidier house and

no more confusion about whether the clothes we see are clean or dirty or what.

3. **Movement:** There are no more pointless trips up and down the stairs to find clothes baskets or to figure out where the dirty clothes ended up. Every trip down to the laundry room or up to the first floor accomplishes something.

4. **Overproduction:** Our laundry demand is much more level than before. We do one load a day, every day. That is always enough and never too much to get done in a day. There are still some problems with it our production levels, though; more on that in moment.

5. **Overprocessing:** Clothes almost never get washed more than once; I rarely neglect to treat them properly beforehand or fail to switch them to the dryer and let it get mildewed.

6. **Transportation:** There is less unnecessary movement of clothes from place to place now. They go down to the laundry room into the sorting baskets, to the machines, to the folding table, and then back up to the closet. That is it.

7. **Waiting:** Clothes get done quicker and more regularly than before. Any article of clothing is likely to get washed within a few days or at most a week, never multiple weeks later like before. This has actually caused a problem by exposing our overproduction of clean clothes. When almost all of our clothes are clean, we

can't fit them all into our closets! Time to do some thinning out.

Taking steps to make a leaner laundry process has paid a lot of dividends, and I have no intention of going back to the other way.

However, the lean production perspective includes the concept of kaizen or continuous improvement. You are never done trying to find ways to eliminate even more waste from any process (and some almost always remains even after a big push to be leaner).

In our case, weekends are a problem. If we skip doing laundry on weekends, loads begin to back up and it takes all week to get rid of the backlog. The simple answer is to do a load every day, even on weekends, but everyone takes weekend trips sometimes. We could do double loads on Mondays and Tuesdays, but it making our process less level is unsustainable. I am still looking for solutions to this problem.

Another problem is dealing with clothes requiring special treatment. Our current system of tying a knot in clothes that require special measures may be hard on garments and doesn't give any information about what treatment is required. A better solution, hopefully not requiring pens and pins and those kinds of things, is out there somewhere.

Chapter 27: Holiday Hangovers Aren't Productive

Over the Christmas holiday weekend, we had visitors in town and did some visiting ourselves. In the meantime, all of the routines we use to keep our lives humming along nicely went out the window. The daily dishwashing, laundry, tidying, etc., that kept our processes leaner and more effective were abandoned for the weekend.

What we are left with is exactly what lean techniques are supposed to eliminate: Large queues (dishes, laundry) waiting for processing, more defects (as washers get overloaded and things get overlooked), etc.

We were entitled some time off, but the result is a reminder that lean methods only work when they are done with creativity, diligence, and discipline. When the cornerstones of lean production are ignored even for a short time, waste creeps back in. Constant vigilance seems to be the only way to combat this weed-like tendency for processes to start accumulating waste.

Luckily, lean techniques provide a ready remedy for such post-break hangovers and in this chapter is a chance to re-apply them with even more care than before. This may even be an opportunity, a chance to re-imagine some of the processes I have worked out as I re-introduce them. Constant improvement is what lean production is all about.

I will begin by getting back to basics and eliminating the most obvious sources of waste in our everyday processes. It's time those dirty dishes left the sink…

One change I have made recently as I attempt to "lean" my everyday life is to run the dishwasher more often. This seems stupid at first glance, since it costs money to run the dishwasher so more running equal more money. In addition, running the dishwasher more frequently (in my case, every night) increases the odds of running it without a full load.

So why am I doing it? Here are some reasons for more-frequent dishwasher runs from a lean perspective:

1. Reducing defects, which are one of the seven muda (types of waste) identified by lean production methods. When we let the washer get over-full, some of the dishes inevitably don't get fully cleaned and we end up having to wash them again in the next run. Cutting down on the load size by upping the frequency largely fixes this.

2. Reducing inventory, another of the seven muda. When we run the dishwasher less often than once a day, we often run out of space and end up having to stack dishes in the sink or on the counter as they wait for space in the washer to open up.

3. Reducing waiting (yes, another of the seven muda). If we can only run the washer when it is full, we inevitably end up waiting around, especially if we are eating out a lot, to finally get it filled up. In the meantime, there are dishes, cutlery, etc., that we cannot use because they are not clean.

These wastes are common in processes where you have not been able to level the demand. Whenever you are dealing with a process where demand unpredictably rises and falls, you will inevitably have some times when resources are sitting idle and other times when you don't have the capacity to meet expectations. These swings, and our attempts to deal with them, inevitably lead to more defects, inventory, and waiting.

One of the goals of lean production methods is to create a more-level demand for the process so these wastes can be reduced. There are various ways of doing this (such as the "heijunka box", which is a simple tool for levelling production), and all of tools are used to try to level demand while still being extremely sensitive to the marketplace and the needs of the customers. It is no small feat.

In the case of my dishwashing, levelling demand is tricky because our use of dishes varies widely from day to day depending on the complexity of meals we are making, the day of the week it is, how often we are eating out, etc. In general, we use somewhat less than a full load of dishes every day.

So I have simply chosen to streamline things as much as I can (such as hand-washing a small number of cups instead of washing them in the dishwasher), and run the dishwasher once a day whether it's full or not. This creates a simple routine where the washer gets loaded before bedtime and unloaded before breakfast, and dirty dishes go right in the washer all day instead of piling up other places.

Levelling out the demand for the dishwasher in this way has eliminated some waste, but not all of it. Although our dishwasher can run a "light" cycle, this only changes the amount of time it is being run. (We are levelling use more than we are truly levelling demand.) Perhaps a better solution for us would be one of the drawer-style washers, since they are configured to run for true half-loads. Unfortunately, we are not ready for a new washer just yet.

So far, a load a day works pretty well, and I am hardly the first to have the idea. It's yet another situation where lean production leads to counter-intuitive results (running the dishwasher more can be more efficient rather than less), which is one reason I find it so fascinating.

Chapter 28: Checking Up On Baby Bottles

Typically, we collect bottles (or actually, sippy cups) throughout the day and then load them into the dishwasher for the overnight load. That made a lot of sense when we were using twenty-four bottles a day.

But now we are just using six bottles a day and those bottles are easier to clean than the earlier ones were because they have many fewer parts. Does it still make sense to keep collecting bottles for the night dishwashing load and do them in one big batch?

Our current baby bottles are also very easy for the kids to make a mess with; squeezing their soft openings against a table or floor or windowsill is apparently the height of fun. So we are going to be switching over to a new, more grownup sippy cup soon. How many should we buy?

If you think about it, the buying question relates directly to the washing question. If we wash bottles in overnight batches, we will need at least six new cups to get us through a day without washing. Those six cups will need to be loaded into the washer, washed, and put back into a cabinet for storage until they are needed (almost twenty four hours later for two of them).

One principle of lean production is that small batches are almost always better than big batches. When you do things in big batches, you get economies of scale (like being able to use the dishwasher rather than doing it by hand), but you lose a lot in terms of flexibility. You also give yourself extra inventory, which has to be stored and maintained somewhere.

Worst of all, you lose some quality control, since if something goes wrong during a big batch run, you won't know about it until the batch is complete, and all of the units in the batch will be affected. I have certainly had the disappointing experience of opening the dishwasher in the morning only to discover that I didn't put in the soap or something, and none of the bottles are clean.

Using small batches has some disadvantages as well, including the loss of some economies of scale and increased changeover times as you switch between batches more frequently. However, these disadvantages can be dealt with through the process of ongoing improvement, which is the core of lean production.

So the answer to my question about baby bottles is clear from a lean perspective. We should buy just two bottles and quickly hand wash them as needed. With that approach, we won't need to set aside an entire cabinet for clean bottle storage, we won't have to spend money on a bunch of extra bottles that spend most of their time not being used, and we will have a much better sense of whether the bottles are being cleaned properly as we are washing them.

It is hard to resist the temptation to buy upwards of a dozen bottles just to save ourselves the momentary task of washing the same two bottles over and over again. Inventory can definitely become a crutch. However, it seems likely that the time we will spend washing two bottles by hand three times a day won't total as much time as it takes to disassemble six bottles, load them into the dishwasher each night, reassemble them in the morning and then move them to the storage cabinet.

Streamlining our baby cups situation by cutting down to just two cups that we would wash by hand replaces our array of more than half a dozen cups that would get washed each night by our dishwasher. This switch makes our cup system consistent with several lean production principles.

- **Smaller batches:** With only two cups ever being dirty, there is no need for the dishwasher's help.
- **Less inventory:** We don't need a whole cabinet to store just two cups.
- **Better quality control:** We can tell right away whether the cups are getting clean or not, rather than waiting overnight.
- **Lower costs:** Two cups are cheaper than a half dozen.
- **"Pull" (on-demand) production:** Cups are only washed when they are needed, not washed and then stored for up to a day at a time before being used.

So far, the new system is working well. I don't even notice the few seconds it takes to clean two cups before they are used. I do notice that the dishwasher has a lot more space available for other things, and that I don't need to set aside time for disassembling and loading six cups before the load starts, or reassembling and storing them when the load finishes. I'm also pondering possible uses for the now-unnecessary cup shelf in the cabinet.

Only two hitches have come up:

1. I have to really keep an eye on the two cups. Toddlers have a tendency to drop cups behind furniture, and with no extras, I can't afford to lose track of them for long.

   As I talked about in a previous chapter, this limitation of resources is actually an advantage. There is nothing worse than finding a several day-old cup of milk going sour under a couch. With no extra cups to turn to when one of them goes missing, I have no freedom to make this sort of mistake and endure the extra labour it would lead to. Running lean takes away the margins that lead to wastefulness.

2. Wear and tear might become an issue. Cups have rubber gaskets that repeated washing may tend to wear down. By washing each cup three or four times a day rather than just once daily, it's possible the cups will wear down three times as fast. I don't see this as a major issue since the kids are developing so fast that they will be graduating to a more mature style of cup soon anyway.

   Even if that was not the case, I feel that the leanest solution would be to totally use up two cups at a time and then replace them with two new cups rather than buy six or eight bottles at the beginning. I am not getting any special deal on cups, and the lean approach argues that inventory is really a cost, not an asset. Best to let the retailer store our replacement cups until we need them rather than store them ourselves.

Chapter 29: Resources Are the Enemy

One common origin story for lean production methods focuses on the Japanese origin of these techniques. Japan has many important manufacturing resources, but is hugely lacking in one. Space. The land in Japan is just too dear to use for massive factories and warehouses, so Japanese manufacturers like Toyota were forced to find a way to manufacture with smaller batches and reduced inventories.

The story makes some sense, but I believe that it tends to miss the point of lean production. In the lean perspective, we have to flip our traditional way of looking at resources and realize that to some extent, having more resources is often part of the problem rather than part of the solution.

If Japanese car companies had enough space to build the kinds of massive factories, warehouses, and dealership lots that characterize American car companies, it would still have been a mistake for them to do so. Having lots of space in your facilities gives you the freedom to be careless. It gives you corners into which you can toss defective parts and forget about them. It gives you floor space to install inflexible, single-purpose machines when better multipurpose solutions might be available. In other words, it gives you room to overlook waste in your operations and do nothing about it.

That isn't to say that resources have no place in lean production. In fact, kaizen (continuous improvement) initiatives often require significant investments of all sorts of resources (time, money, space, personnel) to be successful. (Failure to commit these resources is a big reason why some of these initiatives ultimately fail.) It just means that throwing resources of any kind at a problem can hide underlying waste in the process and prevent it from ever becoming truly lean and smoothly-flowing.

For instance, at home in the past when I got seriously behind on laundry, I did just take a day on the weekend and do nothing but wash and fold clothes. I did use the ample time I had available to compensate for the fact that my laundry wasn't getting done very effectively. The extra time I had to do a weekend laundry blitz blinded me to the fact that my laundry processes were quite wasteful.

Now that I have to drive my son to different activities at the weekend and pick up; I no longer have the extra time for laundry blitzes and have been forced to come to the realization that my laundry process needed revamping. (More on how I did this later.) The thing is, I am not more efficient with laundry because I lack the extra time I had before; I am more efficient because the loss of extra time made me realize the mistakes I had been making all along.

In short, lean methods are not useful only when resources are limited. In fact, the opposite may be true. Organizations that are rich in resources may be more in need of lean-oriented approaches than organizations with fewer resources, which haven't been able to hide from their own wasteful practices as easily.

Being on a small island may have forced Japanese automakers to look closer at their way of doing things, but it is not why Japanese cars are better.

Chapter 30: Non-Lean Doctor's Office

We took our kid to see a specialist today (He is fine), and it showed clearly that despite how widespread lean concepts are becoming, there are many places that have never heard of them and BADLY need to.

On the phone, the clerk made a big deal about how important it was that we arrive early to fill out paperwork, etc. So we actually ran into the building with our son to make sure we were there with plenty of time.

We filled out the paperwork and wait. FORTY-FIVE minutes later, a nurse finally took us to an examination room and took some basic height and weight measurements, checked blood oxygen levels, etc. She then left us in that small room (with nothing to occupy our attention) and said the doctor would be in soon.

We waited a while, and after our son began to melt down through boredom (Children just don't have the ability to wait long periods of time), we went back to the main waiting room, which at least had a TV and space to roam around.

Finally, 2 hours after our appointment began, the doctor finally ushered us back to the examination room. There was no apology or even any acknowledgement that we did spent the last two hours occupying our son in a boring waiting room. He performed the exact same tests (looking in the ears, listening to the chest, etc.) that the nurse had done earlier, and gave us the diagnosis.

The news was good, and my relief almost offset my annoyance at having our time so thoughtlessly wasted. The doctor apparently had been tied up at the hospital, which is why he was so late, but we were not told this until we had been waiting for almost two hours. If we had known, we could have gone to the grocery store or to lunch, but nobody said a word.

The shame is; the doctor was nice. The nurses were nice. The clerks were nice. Nice people and probably fine medical care, but the way we were handled made me feel bad about the whole thing.

It did not have to be this way! There is information all over the place about "lean medical practices," and how they raise profits while increasing patient satisfaction (partly by eliminating waiting and overprocessing like we experienced). Here is one piece about how medical practices can become lean organizations, and there's a lot more where that came from. The information is not hard to find. The only thing that prevents apparently nice and intelligent medical practitioners from learning and applying these ideas is that they simply don't care.

It is understandable; they have a captive market (it is a pain to change Doctors) and no price pressure (who pays attention to what the insurance or the Government pays?), so they feel no need to raise their game. They are not the first industry to feel this way.

They also won't be the first to find out that they are wrong. There is a reason why General Motors is mostly owned by the federal government now. If medicine wants to avoid being socialized, it's time for them to step it up and get lean.

Chapter 31: Conclusion

In my view, the central principle of lean production is that the customer is the focus of everything you do. As you go through the kaizen continuous-improvement process, you subject everything you do to the question. "How does this increase value for the customer?" If something you are doing does nothing to increase value for the customer, or worse, decreases value for the customer, you should try to get rid of it. An ideal lean process would include nothing besides actions that increase value for the customer.

In the case of car companies and other factories, the customer is obvious. The person buying the product that comes from the factory. The reason for maximizing customer value is also obvious. When they have a choice, people don't pay for anything they don't value. If you put things into your process that don't increase value for the customer, you either have to increase prices to pay for them (making a competitor's less-expensive and equally-valuable product more attractive), or you have to pay for them yourself (making your business less profitable). These are both bad.

In everyday life, customers are less obvious partly because they don't usually pay you. In my case, my customers are ultimately myself, my spouse, and my children. None of them pay me for my services, but that doesn't mean that spending my time and energy on actions that don't have value for them is any less of a problem. I want all of these people to have lives that are as full as possible of things they value because I care about them. That is the reason I am trying to make a leaner everyday life: To maximize the value of everything we do.

So lean production is trying to eliminate all of those things that don't have value for the customer, and has a word for those things. Waste. Waste is anything that doesn't add value for the customer. Lean production is a set of tools, techniques and tricks that eliminate waste from the process. At one level, it really is that simple.

Keep improving!!

Resource and References

Shigeo Shingo, Norman Bodek, Collin McLoughlin: Kaizen and the Art of Creative Thinking - The Scientific Thinking Mechanism

Shigeo Shingo; Fundamental Principles of Lean Manufacturing

Shigeo Shingo, Andrew P. Dillon (Translator); Zero Quality Control: Source Inspection and the Poka-yoke System

Shigeo Shingo; Non-Stock Production: The Shingo System of Continuous Improvement

Shigeo Shingo; A Study of the Toyota Production System from an Industrial Engineering Viewpoint

Shigeo Shingo; A Study of the Toyota Production System from an Industrial Engineering Viewpoint

Drucker, P. (1993) Post-Capitalist Society

Drucker, P., "What Makes an Effective Executive", Harvard Business review, June 2004

Lessons from Toyota's long drive, an interview with Katsuaki Watanabe, HBR, July 2007

Liker, J. & D. Meier, Toyota Talent, McGraw Hill, 2007

Shook, J. , Managing To Learn, Lean Enterprise Institute 2008

Fishman, C., "No Satisfaction", Fast Company, Dec 2006/Jan 2007

Womack, J. & J. Shook, Lean Management and The Role of Lean Leadership, Lean Enterprise Institute presentation, Oct. 2006

www.ingramcontent.com/pod-product-compliance
Lightning Source LLC
Chambersburg PA
CBHW060858170526
45158CB00001B/400